THE STORY OF MAPLE LEAF GARDENS

SPORTS PUBLISHING INC.
Champaign Illinois

Director of Production: Susan M. McKinney
Interior Design and Layout: Michelle R. Dressen
Cover Design: Joseph J. Buck

ISBN:1-58261-015-0

Printed in Canada.

For Julie: wife, mother, editor.

ACKNOWLEDGMENTS

My thanks to the employees of Maple Leaf Gardens for their patience, their contributions to this book and for their time during interviews about the Gardens that have appeared in the Toronto Sun the past 12 years.

A special note of gratitude to Paul Morris, for sharing his encyclopedic knowledge of the building and to the Maple Leafs hockey office; Casey Vanden Heuvel, Pat Park and Bob Stellick.

Phil Pritchard and Jane Rodney at the Hockey Hall of Fame went far beyond the call of duty to help compile many of the classic hockey photos. Thanks also to Richard Stromberg at Heritage Toronto and historian/author Mike Filey.

This project could not have begun not been completed without the assistance of the *Toronto Sun* and in particular, Sports Editor Scott Morrison, General Manager Mark Stevens and editor Gary Loewen. Julie Kirsh and the staff of the *Sun* Library were very gracious to let me root through their photo files, some of which I even plan to return.

I'm proud to be associated with so many award-winning *Toronto Sun* and *Toronto Telegram* writers and photographers, whose work is included in these pages.

I only met Stan Obodiac once, but his passion for the team and the building should be appreciated always by Leafs' fans. His books on the Gardens were enormously helpful to me.

Lance Hornby
November 1998
Toronto

CONTENTS

FOREWORD
by Brian Conacher

I grew up with Maple Leaf Gardens.

As a young Leafs fan sitting in the East Rails, seats 69-70. With Foster Hewitt in the gondola. When the ice was scraped with shovels before the Zamboni was invented. As a Junior player with the Marlboros in the late 1950s.

As a Leafs' player in the 1960s.

I remember when the girls fainted for the Beatles and Elvis. Watching Holiday On Ice and Ice Capades. Hearing the lion's roar at the Ringling Brothers Circus and when most of the fans attending hockey games wore dress shirts, ties and jackets.

The Conacher name has been associated with the Gardens since my Uncle Charlie scored the first goal for the Leafs when Conn Smythe opened the doors on Nov. 12, 1931. Uncle Charlie was on the first Leafs team to win a Stanley Cup at the Gardens, while I was fortu-nate enough to wear the Blue & White on the last Stanley Cup team in 1967.

In 1992, when I walked into the Gardens to begin work as Vice-President of

Building Operations for six years, I was still in awe. I had become part of the management of Canada's most legendary and controversial arena. During my tenure, millions were spent to preserve the tradi-tion and history of the Gardens.

Many new arenas have come to the National Hockey League, leaving the Gardens as the only re-maining original building. When the Leafs move to their new age arena in February of 1999, memories will echo through every rafter, seat, dressing room and corridor. If the Gardens could talk, what a story it would tell.

The Gardens is more than just bricks, concrete and steel. It's the people through the years who made it the sports/enterainment mecca it became. Not even 31 years without a Cup could dampen its mystique, charisma and tradition as more than a hockey arena.

Long after the doors close for the final time, the corner of Church and Carlton will always be the home of Maple Leaf Gardens.

Brian Conacher
October, 1998

INTRODUCTION
THE HOUSE THAT CONN BUILT

An estimated 117 million have passed through the doors of Maple Leaf Gardens, as much traffic as some of the world's best known religious shrines.

It's believed every person born in the Greater Toronto Area since 1960 has been there at least once, to see the Leafs or to watch a concert.

The hockey team is going south to a new home and the concert business moved elsewhere long ago. But the largest meeting hall in Canada for six decades will survive in name and spirit, if not as four walls.

"Somehow, through 68 years, it developed a soul, a life of its own," said Bob Stellick, who spent almost 20 years working in various capacities for the Leafs and the Gardens. "It's the ultimate gathering place in Toronto. People identify with it, they know exactly where it is, how to get there and everyone has at least one Gardens

story. It's like your favorite armchair."

That's born out every time the Leafs conducted a fan survey. Complaints are numerous; no air conditioning, no elevators, cramped seating, crowded corridors. But the majority could only agree on one thing–they didn't want to move, despite new rinks popping up all over the National Hockey League.

Somewhere, the man who'd fought incredible odds and public ridicule to give the town a worthy showplace, must be smiling.

Constantine Falkland Kerrys Smythe, Conn to friends and enemies alike, fought for his arena with the same tenacity he showed in sports, school, business and in two world wars.

Born around the corner from where the Gardens would

stand, he made up for lack of size with an aggressive streak in athletics and studies that served him well against the snobs he encountered at posh Upper Canada College.

He won a medal for bravery as an artillery gunner in France during World War I and later joined the Royal Flying Corps. His observation plane was shot down and he spent the last year of the war in a German POW camp.

Smythe came home to complete an engineering degree at the University of Toronto, whose hockey he managed as students and later, as senior players. Smythe's team captured the Allan Cup in 1926 and his reputation spread to New York where the Rangers had just entered the NHL. For $10,000 he took on the job of building the new team. Smythe's famous hockey credo "if you can't beat 'em in the alley, you can't beat 'em on the ice", was operative then, but it was to be the Leafs who would reap its benefits.

He was dropped by the Rangers on the eve of the 1926-27 season, with the owners opting for Lester Patrick, who used many of Smythe's acquisitions to win the Cup that spring.

Using his Rangers' paycheque and cashing in huge winnings on a couple of football and hockey bets, Smythe came home and was back in the NHL in just a few months. He went into partnership with Toronto businessmen J.P. Bickell and Peter G. Campbell, purchasing the Toronto St. Patricks for $160,000 on Valentine's Day 1927.

The St. Pats had won the Cup in 1921-22, but were in decline when Smythe stepped in, just in time to beat an out-of-town buyer from Philadelphia. The St. Pats were playing to poor crowds in the 9,000-seat Arena Gardens on Mutual Street, near their future home.

Smythe quickly chose the name Maple Leafs, which reflected a good soldier's patriotism, adopting the leaf that servicemen wore on their helmets and uniforms as the team's crest.

The Leafs were rapidly becoming a household word, thanks to pioneering broadcaster Foster Hewitt, who'd called the first-ever game on radio from Mutual Street in 1923.

Smythe wasted no time building a contender. He packaged a group of veterans to Detroit for $75,000 and brought in goalie Lorne Chabot, winger Harold (Baldy) Cotton and centre Andy Blair.

Then came the Kid Line of Busher Jackson, Joe Primeau and Charlie Conacher in 1929, joining the fiery Red Horner. The biggest coup came early in the 1930-31 season, when colorful defenceman King Clancy was purchased from the cash strapped Ottawa Senators.

The club's directors first vetoed the outlandish price of $35,000 for Clancy, but Smythe solved that in one afternoon at Woodbine race track, with $60 on a long shot he owned called Rare Jewel. By that night, Smythe had another $15,000 to throw in the Clancy pot and with two Toronto players added to the package, the deal was done.

But Mutual Street was now hopelessly unable to handle the demand for tickets. The Leafs either had to get out of the cramped arena or leave town altogether. The onset of the Depression in 1929-30 posed obvious problems. Financing a new building now seemed suicidal, making Smythe's partners queasy about any plan to leave Mutual Street.

But Smythe's powers as a salesman and motivator would not be denied. The call for a new showplace for sports and the arts in town was already well supported and Smythe, intrigued by stories from New York about Carnegie Hall and the new Empire State Building, believed Toronto should have its own landmark edifice. Smythe initially had two sites in mind; Yonge Street where it kissed the waterfront and Knox College on Spadina Crescent. But the owners of the former wanted too high a price and residents near the latter didn't want their neighborhood 'spoiled' by a sports arena.

It was in the autumn of 1930, that an underpriced lot running 350 feet on Carlton Street and 282 feet north on Church caught Smythe's eye. It intersected two streetcar lines, was a stone's throw from busy Yonge Street, and best of all was cheap at $350,000.

The land was owned by department store giant, the T. Eaton Co., which was anxious for development to enhance its new store a block away at College Street and Yonge. But highbrow Eaton's president J.J. Vaughan was initially against the Gardens project.

"The people who atend sporting events were hardly the type Eaton's catered to," recalled Frank Selke, Smythe's assistant.

But Smythe quickly spread the word he was

going to build "the finest looking and best planned indoor sports centre in North America."

The prominent Montreal architectural firm of Ross and Macdonald were hired, already well known in Toronto for completing big projects on time, such as Union Station, the Royal York Hotel and Mutual Street.

Smythe decided to call his dream palace Maple Leaf Gardens, borrowed from Madison Square Garden in New York. A hundred years ago, the original MSG was a roofless hippodrome known as Gilmore's Garden, with flowers, walkways, and a naughty element, spiced by illegal boxing.

Armed with the first drawings of his Gardens, Smythe commissioned the bright young Selke to create a 10-cent program that would attract fan interest and new investors. When Hewitt mentioned Selke's project on the air, almost 100,000 replies came back, many with a dime carefully tucked in. The response elated Smythe, and boosted the di-

rectors sagging confidence. A prospectus was created and people were drawn to Smythe's pep talks on the advantages of owning a piece of a building with sellout potential for hockey, in a high traffic area, front by a dozen stores.

Smythe and Selke made sure well-to-do female fans received copies of the prospectus, for their own investments or to influence their sports-minded husbands.

On February 24, 1931, Maple Leaf Gardens Ltd. was incorporated, the board including such heavyweights as Sir John Aird, president of the Bank of Commerce, and Alf Rogers, president of St. Mary's Cement. A $500,000 mortgage with Sun Life Assurance was arranged, 100,000 prefered shares at $10 were offered and 50,000 common shares at $3.

The houses and tobacco shops that front Church and Carlton began to be cleared, but almost immediately there was another crisis for Smythe. At a meeting to open the contractor's bids

First Family: In 1970, Gardens founder Conn Smythe poses with grandson Tom, who is holding his son, Thomas Brent, with Conn's son Stafford on the right.

at Aird's office on King Street, it was determined the board was still several hundred thousand dollars short of financing its $1.5 million project.

It was Selke to the rescue again. As business manager of the electricians union, Selke knew the Allied Building Trades Coucil was having its weekly meeting that day on Church Street.

Selke hurried over and explained what the postponement or cancellation of the Gardens would mean to workers already hit by lean times. Selke, whose mortgage was tied up in Gardens' fundraising, was ultimately successful in talking all 24 unions into taking 20% of their pay in Gardens stock.

Those shares reached $100 in value by 1947 and split four to one, then five to one in 1965. A few shares remained in the hands of the workers on their heirs as late as the 1990s when the company went private.

Thomson Brothers Construction of Toronto broke ground for the Gardens in late May and an army that would grow to 1,300 workers descended on the site.

Where Skydome would take close to two years to build with 1980s technology, the Gardens was ready to host hockey in an astounding 5½ months. In retrospect, Smythe was not surprised at the speed.

"Partly it was accomplished because the men who built it believed in what they were doing," he wrote later.

From six story elevations that border Church, Carlton and Wood Streets, the building rose to 15 stories in the centre, with 13 million cubic feet of space. Wrapped in yellow-gold brick with walls as thick as 25 inches of reinforced concrete, the exterior mixed features of Art Deco and Art Moderne.

As the crowd of 13,233 made their way in, some men in top hats and ladies in furs, the 48th Highlanders and the Royal Grenadiers struck up "Happy Days Are Here again." 'History in the making,' the Toronto Telegram reported.

"You can come to 50 games a year here and still get a thrill of that first sight of the ice," Gardens oldtimers are fond of saying. "Coming through from the hall to see the clock, the stands, the big roof, the two teams and all that color ... it still sends a tingle up your spine."

About the Author . . .

Lance Hornby has covered the Maple Leafs and the National Hockey League for the Toronto Sun since 1986. He has covered a wide range of beats during 17 years at the Sun with a brief stop at the Toronto Star in 1981. In addition to the Leafs, his assignments have included the Toronto Blue Jays, the CFL Argonauts and local amateur sports. Hornby lives in his native Toronto with his wife, Julie, and their children, Dylan and Kate.

The Toronto Sun, flagship of the Sun Media Corp., is the second-largest daily newspaper group in Canada in terms of circulation. For more information, call 416/947-2222 or visit the internet version of the Toronto Sun at www.canoe.ca.

1

OPENING NIGHT/November 12, 1931

The Leafs lost the game, their president was almost arrested and an impatient crowd nearly booed the politicians off the ice during long-winded pre-game ceremonies.

But such irritations couldn't cloud the night the Leafs and the city came of age.

The largest crowd to watch a sporting event in Toronto to that time crammed into 13,233 seats, with Conn Smythe and his directors beaming under their top hats.

It was a different story for Smythe earlier that day. In his effort to eavesdrop on people in the ticket lines to get true impressions of the new palace and to weed out scalpers, he'd jumped from queue to queue and caught the attention of a suspicious policeman. He was escorted off the premises until he could prove his identity.

The top ticket for

boxes and rails was $3, down to a buck for end greens, blues and greys. A program was 15 cents and folks marvelled at the two-lane bowling alley, the billiards room, the small gymnasium, soft drinks served in cups and the precarious perch of Foster Hewitt's gondola.

The Leafs and the Chicago Blackhawks skated out for warmups at 8:30 p.m., the cue for the 48th Highlanders and the Royal Grenadiers band in the north end to strike up the anti-Depression tune, "Happy Days Are Here Again".

Lengthy opening ceremonies began with a floral horseshoe tribute to the Leafs from Mayor William J. Stewart and city council. J.P. Bickell, representing the Gardens,

The program cover from Maple Leaf Gardens' opening night.

saluted a building that was "entirely Canadian, in conception, plan, design and material", earning some cheers.

But from the greys, which didn't have as much tux-and-tails refinement, came shouts of "play hockey" during Bickell's address.

Smythe was later to recall glancing around the Gardens during the speeches, surveying the faces of many men who'd built it, those who held stock and those who had sold and were just starting to realize what they'd surrendered.

The Mayor had a turn at the microphone, as well as Chicago captain Cy Wentworth, but fewer and fewer were in a mood to listen. When Premier George S. Henry's turn came, a heckler shouted "wider highways!" to a few laughs, all of which prompted the Telegram to admonish the "rabble" and their manners.

The Highlanders played the Maple Leaf Forever, for the first of 68 consecutive home openers, and the game finally began. King Clancy threw the first bodycheck, but the nervous Leafs gave up the first goal at 2:30 of the opening period.

Harold (Mush) March, who'd already made local history for scoring the last goal on Mutual St., took a pass from Tommy Cook and flipped the puck over Lorne Chabot. Taffey Abel of Chicago took the first penalty. Chicago's Chuck Gardiner

was having a fine game in goal, until a violent collision after a save on Charlie Conacher in the second period. Writhing in agony from a badly bruised arm, Gardiner was the first visitor to the Gardens clinic.

With no backup in those days, the game was held up 10 minutes until Gardiner could continue. Conacher, who had been trying for the far corner all night, finally succeeded getting past the Hawks' defence at 18:42 of the period, burying a Joe Primeau pass.

A solo rush by Vic Ripley paid off in a goal at 2:35 of the third, all Chicago would need after a major to Primeau late in the game for "accidentally raising a bump" on Tom Cook's forehead, according to the Tely.

But the score in the debut was secondary to reviews of the building in the following day's Tely. The clear sightlines and ventilation drew high praise and police officials expressed amazement that almost 14,000 spectators could be dispersed from the building in a little more than five minutes.

"Toronto has grown up, out of the bush leagues and into the big time," began the Tely's story.

From now on, the corner of Church and Carlton was the crossroads of hockey in Canada.

First Home: The Mutual St. Arena, original home of the Leafs, located a few blocks from the future Gardens.

Before the Roar: Carlton St., looking east to Church St., in the 1920s. (Mike Filey)

Future Site: Stores and houses on the north side of Carlton St. where the Gardens now stands. (Mike Filey)

GARDENS EVENTS—1931

NOV. 12 - Opening night, 1931-32 season; Chicago 2, Toronto 1; NOV. 13, First OHA senior game, Nationals 3. Marlboros 2; NOV. 16, First junior game, Toronto Canoe Club 10, U of T Schools 0; NOV. 19, Queensbury Athletic Club wrestling; NOV. 28, First Leafs win at Gardens, 4-3 over Boston; DEC. 6, First Leafs shutout, 4-0 over Montreal Maroons.

Breaking Ground: Ground is broken for the building of Maple Leaf Gardens. Conn Smythe's sand and gravel company did much of the work. Smythe is somwhere in the crowd in this photo. (Paul Morris)

Beginning phase of construction of the Gardens. (Paul Morris)

(Paul Morris)

(Paul Morris)

(Paul Morris)

(Paul Morris)

(Paul Morris)

(Paul Morris)

The pipes for ice are shown in this photo. (Paul Morris)

Gardens Events—1932

MARCH 3, Winston Churchill speech; APRIL 9, Leafs defeat Rangers 6-4 to win first of 11 Stanley Cups; MAY 2, Lions Club boxing; MAY 3, Ontario Lacrosse League opens, Maple Leafs 12, Tecumsehs 5; MAY 4, Pro badminton tournament; MAY 12-13, Olympic boxing exhibition; MAY 19, Boxing, Al Brown def. Spider Pladner; OCT. 24, Mann Cup Lacrosse, Mimico beats Winnipeg 16-6 in final; NOV. 10, 1932-33 home opener, Leafs 1, Bruins 1.

Gardens Events—1933

JAN. 21, Leafs beat four senior OHA teams in charity exhibition; FEB. 7, Public skating; APRIL 3, Ken Doraty ends game at 104:46 of overtime; APRIL 4, Bill Tilden tennis challenge; MAY 5, Jehovah's Witnesses; NOV. 9, 1933-34 home opener, Leafs 6, Boston 1; DEC. 7, Upper Canada College alumni game; DEC. 21, Wrestling.

Gardens Events—1934

JAN. 11,Wrestling; FEB. 6-7, North American speed skating finals; FEB. 14, Ace Bailey benefit game; MARCH 17, King Clancy Night; MARCH 31, Allan Cup final, Moncton 3, Fort William 2; APRIL 7, International hockey, Detroit 2, Moncton 1; APRIL 27, Independent Order Of Foresters pageant; APRIL 28, Toronto Girl Guides rally;MAY 15-16, Toronto Catholic School Board pageant; MAY 21-22, Dominion boxing championships; MAY 24, Toronto Boy Scouts rally; JUNE 9, wrestling; JULY 8, Jehovah's Witnesses; SEPT. 7, Aimee Semple McPherson; SEPT. 19, Oddfellows convention; SEPT. 21, Eddie Duchin dance concert; OCT. 18, Wrestling; OCT. 21-27, Six-day bicycle races; NOV. 8, 1934-35 home opener, Leafs 5, Boston 3; NOV. 20, Busher Jackson's four-goal period vs. St. Louis; DEC. 2, Toronto and District Labour Forum; DEC. 22, Young Canada Night; DEC. 31; Don Retman Orchestra.

Gardens Gallery • A Job Well Done

It took 1,300 workers to build the Gardens, beginning with the demoliton of the stores at Church and Carlton on April 1, 1931. Actual construction began around June 1 and it opened an astonishing 5½ months later.

The materials used in construction included 760 tons of structural steel, 750,000 bricks, 77,500 bags of cement, 1,100 tons of gravel, 70 tons of sand, 950,000 feet of lumber, 230,000 haylite blocks and 540 kegs of nails. The finished product was a 350 by 282-foot building that rises 13 stories and contains 13,000,000 cubic feet of space.

With materials costing up to 30% less because of the low demand in the Depression, few delays occured and no brick, nail, lumber or pebble seems to have gone unused.

2

THE 1967 CUP

Just before the young generation ushered in The Summer Of Love in 1967, the aging Maple Leafs had one more spring fling with the Stanley Cup.

The images of captain George Armstrong scoring into an empty Montreal net, coach Punch Imlach's high tilted fedora and the dented profiles of Terry Sawchuk and Johnny Bower remain sharp as ever in a city that has never tasted a title since.

"I'd won the Cup before," Bower said, "but '67 will always stand out because of us older players. There was a definite feeling that some of us would never get a chance at another."

Bower was prophetic. Only Frank Mahovich, Larry Hillman and Mike Walton ever sipped from the Cup again.

If everyone likes an underdog, there was so much to love about the '67 Leafs. Tim Horton, Bower and Stanley were in their 40s and the average age on the Leafs was 31.2. Far from being wire-to-wire champions, they were plagued by injuries. Ron Ellis's 22 goals were the lowest of any Cup winner, the team lost 10 straight at mid-season, still a franchise record, and a drained Imlach briefly checked into hospital.

In the first round, the Leafs drew Chicago, the day's most dreaded foe. But Bower and Sawchuk weathered Bobby Hull and Stan Mikita in a six-game shocker.

Sawchuk was especially brilliant, despite head to toe injuries.

"That was the bigger upset," insisted defenceman Marcel Pronovost. "But everyone remembers Montreal the next round."

It was the NHL's last Original Six series, the Flying Frenchmen and the Lunchbucket Leafs, Two Solitudes with the backdrop of Confederation's 100th anniversary and Montreal's Expo '67.

Not even the Hockey Night In Canada TV crews were doing the traditional mix and match, with Montreal's Danny Gallivan and Dick Irvin deciding it best to steer clear of Bill Hewitt and Co.

But someone on the Montreal side of the fence made the mistake of saying how nice the Stanley Cup looked at Expo's Quebec Pavilion where the 1966 champions had loaned it for display.

"When we heard that, we decided to get it for the Ontario Pavilion," Pronovost said.

Imlach stressed a choking checking system that forced Montreal to the outside and made up for the Leafs' lack of speed.

"We felt we had a twin for a shadow," Jean Beliveau complained.

Imlach worked with four primary defencemen and used the line of Bob Pulford, Jim Pappin and Peter Stemkowski to stymie the swift Habs. The Leafs won two of three games at the Gardens, Game 3 in double overtime on a Pulford goal and of course, the clincher on May 2.

Ellis and Pappin scored second-period goals that night, Dick Duff narrowed it for the Habs and

Last Title Taste: Captain George Armstrong cradles the 1967 Cup at the Gardens. The Leafs upset Chicago and Montreal with a hard-working team. (Hockey Hall of Fame)

with a minute to go and Montreal coach Toe Blake pulled Gump Worsley with a faceoff in the Leafs end.

Imlach sent out his entire old guard; Armstrong, Red Kelly, Horton, Allan Stanley and Bob Pulford, instructing Stanley to take a rare draw. The defenceman was shocked, but won the faceoff and tied up Beliveau so Armstrong could score.

"It was the most spontaneous cheer I've heard in all my (49) years here," veteran usher Dennis

Goodwin said. "I'd snuck in a bottle of champagne and was serving everyone in my section in the greens in Dixie cups."

Imlach called it his most rewarding Cup.

"They may not have been the best players," the demanding coach would often say, "but they never quit, never let me beat them and they sure as hell weren't going to let the other team win."

Gardens Gallery • Hal-Mark theatre

It's said Harold Ballard had his fingerprints on everything at the Gardens and in some places there is tangible proof.

When the Gardens laid down a new cement floor in 1983, Ballard put his handprints and name at centre ice, as a permanent memorial to himself. He also put his initials in the foundations for a new compressor in the ice plant in 1980.

In another Ballard tradition that continued into his 80s, he made sure he was the first on the ice every autumn when a new sheet was put in and got to take the last lap every spring before the ice was torn up.

DARRYL SITTLER SCORES 10 POINTS
in 11-4 Win Over Boston/February 7, 1976

It was once predicted that Darryl Sittler's record 10-point game would still be safe when they played the Stanley Cup on Mars.

No one from the red planet has communicated with the NHL's expansion committee as of yet, but the greatest one-game points binge in league history is still safe heading into the millennium.

Wayne Gretzky is running out of time, Mario Lemieux has moved on, expansion teams and more than a few sieve goalies have come and gone. But the stars may never be aligned as they were at the Gardens that night.

"It's a record Wayne Gretzky doesn't have—yet," Sittler said on the 20th anniversary of his six goals and four assists. There are about 250 Leafs who've never had that many points in their Toronto careers, never mind one night.

"I could study the replays of that game again and again," Sittler said. "But as much as people fault (Bruins' goalie) Dave Reece, it was just a night where every pass and every shot somehow found their way to the right place.

"Reece was screened a couple of times, but I don't think he flubbed one goal.

"Look at my face (on highlights) on the 10th point. When I tried to pass in front, it hit Brad Park's skate and went in. That smile and a shrug say it all."

There wasn't a hint of anything special in the air that night, in fact the new captain had drawn the wrath of Harold Ballard that week for scoring just once in his previous eight games.

Before the game, Lanny McDonald recalled having to talk coach Red Kelly out of breaking up he, Sittler and Errol Thompson because the coach felt all the scoring was concentrated on one line.

McDonald ended up with a goal and three assists, Thompson three assists.

Bruins' coach Don Cherry unwittingly helped by his decision on a starting goaltender.

Gerry Cheevers had just returned to Boston from the WHA, but Cherry wanted to keep him fresh for a big homecoming and let rookie Reece face the Leafs.

Riding a seven-game winning streak, Cherry thought the risk was worth it. He wouldn't switch as Sittler's carnage mounted, two assists in the first period, a hat trick and two helpers in the second, a hat trick in the third.

Sittler used to joke that Reece tried to throw himself in front of a subway car that night "but it went through his legs."

But Reece dropped off the face of the earth after that season and Sittler felt bad he never had a chance to talk to him. It wasn't until the summer of 1995 that he happened to meet Reece's niece, who recognized Sittler in the crowd at a sporting event in Lake Placid, N.Y.

"He's teaching school in Rhode Island or somewhere in New England," Sittler said. "I hope he's doing well for himself."

A Perfect 10: Darryl Sittler's fourth of his six goals in his NHL Record 10-point night. (Toronto Sun)

Gardens Events—1935

MARCH 5, Interfaith church service; MARCH 22, Maple Leaf track meet; APRIL 19, Pro tennis; SEPT. 22-28, Six-day bicycle races; OCT. 6, Salvation Army meeting; OCT. 8 Admiral Richard Byrd lecture; OCT. 8, Liberal party rally; OCT. 9, Conservative Party rally; OCT. 11, Reconstruction Party rally; OCT. 12; Economic Forum; OCT. 25-26, ballet; OCT. 28-NOV. 2, Shrine Circus; NOV. 9 1935-36, home opener, Leafs 5, NY Americans 5: NOV. 13; Joe Louis boxing exhibition; NOV. 27, Five Pianos ensemble.

Gardens Gallery • Snack Attack

On opening night in 1931, patrons thought they were in the lap of luxury when soft drinks were served in cups.

Selection remained limited, but by the late 1950s, there were eskimo pies and boxed popcorn for a dime and hot dogs for 15 cents.

In the 1990s, fans could grumble about the cost, but not the variety. In addition to an average Saturday game when 2,100 units of popcorn, 2,000 ice cream bars and 1,800 hot dogs were consumed, fans had other favorites to munch on. They included pizza (1,300 slices a game), peanuts (750 bags), chocolate bars (700), nachos (400 four-ounce boxes), potato chips (350 bags), soft pretzels (350) and deli sandwiches (200).

To wash it down, about 10,000 cups of beer are poured a night, 350 cups of wine, 5,100 pops and 1,100 juices, mineral waters and iced teas.

More food is also consumed on Saturdays at the Gardens, especially after the change in time for home games in the 1990s saw many fans skip supper.

4

FIRST CUP—APRIL 9, 1932

One of the clever marketing ploys to get public support behind construction of the Gardens was that the Bruins, Rangers and Montreal Maroons had all won Stanley Cups in the late 1920s in the first year they moved into new buildings.

The prophecy came true for the Leafs on this day when they completed a high-scoring sweep of the Rangers with a 6-4 win before 14,366 at the Gardens.

The city had waited 10 years for the Cup to come back. It was the first time a Cup winner had taken the best-of-five final in three straight. The Rangers were the more well-rested team when the series began, but Jackson knocked the stuffing out of them with a three-goal game in the opener.

A circus at Madison Square Garden forced Game 2 to Boston where the Leafs won easily. In the clincher, the Kid Line of Conacher, Primeau and Jackson was in on the six straight goals, but defencemen Hap Day and Andy Blair (two goals) had the strongest game according to reports.

Smythe had been richly rewarded for his Gardens gamble and the fact he'd humbled the team that fired him made victory all that sweeter. The players presented him with an expensive stop watch for his burgeoning racing stable and Smythe in turn named three new thoroughbreds Stanley Cup, Six-To-Four and Three Straight.

The city gave each Leaf an illuminated scroll, local clothing firms showered them with gifts and the club awarded each man a gold medal.

Toronto coach Dick Irvin, avenging his loss as Chicago coach in the '31 final, had to leave town quickly after the win, to attend to his sick infant son back home in Western Canada. More than 40 years later, Dick Irvin Jr., became a Hall Of Fame broadcaster.

New Home of Champions: No sooner did the Leafs move into the Gardens then they won the 1931-32 Cup as Conn Smythe had predicted. (Hockey Hall of Fame)

BILL BARILKO/1951 CUP

His No. 5 hangs from the rafters, the tribute song "Fifty Mission Cap" is played at least once every home game and the picture of his 1951 Cup-winning goal at the Gardens still draws a crowd.

Though 'Bashing Bill' didn't quite have the credentials of the great Leafs, he's larger than life nearly 50 years after his tragic death.

One of the most rambunctious defencemen of his day, with a minor league career that took him to a team in Hollywood, Barilko usually was disoriented on the other side of centre. That is, until April 21, 1951, when the 24-year-old soared like Superman and delivered the Cup-winning goal. It capped an incredible five-game series against the Canadiens, in which every match went into overtime.

The Leafs were headed for a one-goal loss in regulation until Todd Sloan scored with Turk Broda on the bench with just 32 seconds to play. At 2:53 of overtime, Barilko somehow sensed he had to move up on a Leafs rush and got a weak Harry Watson pass at the top of the faceoff circle. He flung himself into a shot that stunned Habs goalie Gerry McNeil over the right shoulder.

It was Barilko's first and only brush with Cup heroics. Late that summer, concluding a fishing trip with a friend from his home town of Timmins, their single engine plane disappeared en route home from James Bay.

The search continued on and off until the bodies were recovered 11 years later, in bush 60 miles north of Cochrane. The Leafs promptly ended their Cup drought, adding more to the mystique of Barilko.

His number and Ace Bailey's No. 6 are the only two Leaf sweaters officially retired, though Bailey's was activated for Ron Ellis in the 1960s. No one has worn No. 5 since Barilko's celebrated goal and tragic death.

Gardens Events—1936

JAN. 7; Canadian Olympic Hockey exhibition; JAN. 21, Leafs - Canadiens game cancelled after death of King George V; JAN. 28, Memorial service for the King; FEB. 19; Boxing; MARCH 20, Track and field meet; APRIL 13, Memorial Cup, West Toronto 4, Saskatoon 2; APRIL 22, Boxing; APRIL 24, IOF pageant; APRIL 27-MAY 2, Six day bicycle race; MAY 18, Olympic boxing trials; MAY 22, boxing; Aug. 2; model airplane show; OCT. 2, Mann Cup lacrosse final, Orillia 10, Vancouver 8; OCT. 14, opera; OCT. 18, Toronto Symphony; OCT. 19, boxing; OCT. 21, opera; OCT. 26-31, Shrine Circus; NOV. 5, 1936-37 home opener, Detroit 3, Leafs 1; NOV.18, church meeting

Gardens Events—1937

JAN. 6, boxing; APRIL 2, boxing; APRIL 17, international hockey, Wembley (England) 6, Hershey Bears 3; APRIL 18, Memorial Cup final, Winnipeg 7, Copper Cliff 0; APRIL 19, international hockey, Wembley 4, Winnipeg 2; APRIL 23, pro tennis; APRIL 26, international hockey, Sudbury def. Wembley; APRIL 30, IOF pageant; MAY 1, Labour conference; MAY 8, Girl Guides rally; MAY 19, Lacrosse; JUNE 1, Boxing; OCT. 25-30, Shrine Circus; NOV. 4, 1937-38 home opener, Leafs 2, Detroit 2.

6

THE BEATLES—September 7, 1964

Of all the mismatches at the Gardens through the years, perhaps the worst was the Beatles and their puny microphones against 18,000 screaming teenagers.

"Imagine the loudest thunder clap you ever heard," the *Telegram*'s Frank Tumpane reported after the first of two concerts. "Imagine that it emanates inside a building and then imagine it's pitched as high as a siren."

The noise didn't abate, from the previous day when the Fab Four landed at the airport, to their drive to the King Edward Hotel, to their trip to the Gardens in a police paddywagon, with 1,000 officers on crowd control duty. Tickets had been sold in a frenzy months before, disrupting the Stanley Cup play-offs. Leafs' great Charlie Conacher even tried to pull strings to secure a pair for his family.

Introduced by local DJs Jay Nelson and Al Boliska, the Beatles played about half an

Yeah, Yeah, Yeah: The Beatles on stage at the Gardens.

hour, long enough for between 100 and 200 kids to require medical aid for exhaustion or what was described as "Beatle Shock".

"All you think about today were those kids screaming," sound man Paul Morris recalled of John, Paul, George and Ringo. "The funny thing was, we had to rush down after the first show, disconnect their mikes and set them up in the Hot Stove Lounge for their press conference, because they were the only mikes we had."

Derek Taylor, the Beatles' irreverent press officer, opened the Hot Stove session by reading a telegram from a man in Saskatchewan who wanted the Beatles' bath water for commercial uses and another huckster who sought their tonsils. Lennon, who was earlier talked into re-naming Hamilton Mountain, Beatle Mountain was asked what time he got up in the morning, and quipped "two in the afternoon." Irked by another question about how long the Beatles would

last, he shot back at the reporter "longer than you."

Toronto was Canadian headquarters for the Beatles Fan Club, thus assuring a raucous welcome, while George Harrison met relatives who lived in town. All manner of fans and phoneys tried to sneak into the King Eddy and the Gardens during that crazy day.

The Beatles' second of three visits to the Gardens in 1965 pitted their hot-tempered manager, Brian Epstein, against the crafty Harold Ballard and Stafford Smythe. The Beatles were scheduled to do only one show, but smelling six-figure profits, the duo sold tickets for an afternoon show.

Epstein went nuts and threatened to cancel everything, but Ballard had him escorted to the Hot Stove for a soothing drink and the Beatles staved off a riot and agreed to the second show. Legend has it Ballard shut off the water taps that hot August day, to drive thirsty patrons to overpriced concession stands.

Harrison and Paul McCartney would return to the Gardens in the 1970s with solo acts.

Hot Stove Beatles: The press conference in the Hot Stove after the 1964 concert.

THE 1942 RALLY CUP

Any time an NHL playoff team falls behind 3-0 in a best-of- seven series, you can bet one sign in their arena will read: "Remember The '42 Leafs".

They were the first team in pro sports to win a championship series after losing the first three games and almost 60 years later, remain the only NHL squad to do it in the Cup final. In the darkest days of World War II, the comeback electrified the whole nation. The largest crowd to watch a hockey game in Canada up to then, 16,218, jammed inside for the 3-1 win.

Facing disaster early in the series at the hands of the underdog Red Wings, Leafs coach Hap Day used every motivational trick in the book. He benched stars Gordie Drillon and Bucko McDonald, he waved newspaper clippings that predicted a Detroit sweep and, after Game 3, he read a letter from a 14-year-old girl who implored her favorite team not to give up.

Bill MacBrien, a Gardens director, got in on the act, deliberately trashing the Leafs between Games 3 and 4, in the hope Detroit would get overconfident.

The Wings' commanding lead early in the series was a tribute to wily Jack Adams, their coach. Common strategy of the era was to carry the puck almost end to end, but Adams figured if Detroit simply iced it (there was no centre red line yet) it could swarm slow-footed Leafs such as McDonald and score off turnovers.

Detroit won 3-2, 4-2 and 5-2 and it seemed the Leafs were coming apart, including the great Turk Broda in net. But in Game 4, the tide turned. Don Metz, who had two goals all year, replaced Drillon, the team's leading scorer. Rookie defenceman Ernie Dickens was also promoted over McDonald, both contributing to a 4-3 win. Detroit began to falter, starting with Adams being suspended for attacking the referee after Game 4.

Metz, playing on a line with brother Nick and Syl Apps, scored three in Game 5 at the Gardens, a 9-3 romp.

The Wings showed signs of life in Game 7 with a 1-0 lead, but Pete Langelle's go-ahead goal in the third was the backbreaker in the eventual 3-1 win.

Comeback kids: Pete Langelle's goal helps clinch the '42 Cup. (Hockey Hall of Fame)

8

PUNCH IMLACH

The image of Punch Imlach's fedora bobbing behind the Leafs bench is as much a part of building lore as Vince Lombardi on the sidelines of Lambeau Field, more than 30 years after his fourth and final Cup.

How different hockey history may have turned out in this town under Imlach's original plan of letting a guy named Alf Pike coach the team at the dawn of the '60s.

Pike, the former Ranger, was approached by Imlach to go behind the bench in 1958-59 when the latter took over as general manager. But Pike wanted too many provisions in his contract and Imlach, either impatient, ambitious or both, went ahead and replaced the struggling Billy Reay with himself on November 29, 1958.

Four Cups— and 365 regular

Plenty O'Punch: Imlach in classic pose behind the Leafs' bench.

season wins later, Imlach was proved right. Ask his players, who largely detested his autocratic behavior, but knew he could push the right buttons.

Imlach first learned how to get maximum results from his conscripts as a second lieutenant during World War II and then as the successful GM of the minor league Quebec Aces for a decade.

He didn't think twice about coming home to Toronto when Stafford Smythe approached him about the Leafs assistant GM's position. He grew up a short ride from the Gardens, just across the Don in Riverdale. His father was a Toronto Transit Commission worker who had served in World War I in the 48th Highlanders.

Imlach was completely unknown at the Gardens, where office secretaries first mistook this plain-looking 40-year-old as a visitor. It was a bizarre situation in that Imlach and Clancy both held the assistant's title with no GM to assist. Smythe was a businessman and Reay refused the dual-role.

It took a terrible start to the 1958-59 season—just five wins approaching December 1—for Imlach to make his move.

Imlach got permission from the panicky board of directors to sack Reay and coach the team himself. His strong knowledge of the hockey grapevine allowed him to add Carl Brewer, Allan Stanley, Larry Regan and Gerry Ehman to the team.

His infectious optimism did the rest that year, as he told anyone who listened the Leafs still would make the '59 playoffs. Even the bold Conn Smythe thought the new coach was nuts. But from the huge hole the Leafs had dug themselves in the autumn, they made up nine points with five games to play and went all the way to the final against Montreal.

The stage was set for a wonderful 10 years in club annals.

Gardens Gallery • Ticket Price Chart

1931-32

Boxes	blues	end greens	greys	end blue/greys
$3.00	$1.50	$1.00	$1.25	$1.00

1941-42

$3.00	$2.50	$1.75	.90	.60

1951-52

$3.50	$2.50	$1.25	$1.50	.75

1961-62

Boxes/rails	blues	greens	greys	general adm. greys
$4.50	$3.50	$2.50	$1.50	1.00.

1971-72

$7.70	$6.60	$4.95	$3.30	$3.30

1981-82

Golds	reds	blues	greens	greys	standing room
$15.00	$12.00	$9.00	$7.00	$5.00	$5.00

1991-92

$40.00	$35.00	$25.00	$22.00	$16.00	$16.00

1998-99

$121.00	$93.00	$53.00	$53.00	$26.50	$26.50

9

1962 CUP

All the ingredients of a champion were there for Imlach, a high-scoring winger in Frank Mahovlich, tireless Dave Keon at centre, Tim Horton, Allan Stanley and Bob Baun on defence, goaltending and youth sprinkled throughout the lineup.

The road to the Leafs' first Cup in 11 years went through New York and Chicago, their first Cup showdown since the Blackhawks beat them in 1938.

The only overtime game of the entire playoffs was April 5, in Game 5 of the knotted series with the Rangers. Red Kelly delighted the Gardens faithful at 4:23 of the second extra frame for the 3-2 win, poking in a puck that was underneath Gump Worsley's head.

The Blackhawks were the defending champions, but Toronto used its Gardens advantage to establish a 2-0 series lead. Captain George Armstrong had four points in those games, including the Game 2 winner with four minutes to play.

Johnny Bower was the Leafs' signature goaltender, but when he was hurt in Chicago and the Hawks tied the series it was up to Don Simmons, who'd been used sparingly that year. However, the Leafs put on a stunning display of power to protect Simmons with an 8-4 win.

Back in Chicago, the Hawks took a 1-0 lead midway through the third period of Game 6 on a Bobby Hull goal, but the resulting shower of debris caused a long delay that helped the Leafs regain momentum. Bob Nevin tied it and with six minutes to play, Dick Duff took Tim Horton's picture pass, a playoff record 13th assist for the latter, and beat Glenn Hall for the winner.

The 1962 Cup Winner, the first of three straight. (Hockey Hall of Fame)

10

1963 CUP

It came on the heels of the Leafs' only regular season title in the past 50 years, edging Chicago 82 points to 81. The Leafs allowed just 180 goals for a second straight year and rode a 73-point year from Mahovlich and fellow all-star team members Horton and Brewer. Kent Douglas won the Calder, Keon captured his second Lady Byng Trophy.

But it was Bower who led the way once play-offs commenced as the Leafs lost just twice that spring. With two shutouts against the powerful Habs, he spear-headed the Leafs into a Cup final against Detroit.

The Wings never quite recov-ered from a master-ful performance by Dick Duff in Game 1 at the Gardens when he exploded from the opening faceoff for two goals in the first 68 seconds. Duff,

Nevin, Stewart, Kelly and Keon all had multiple-goal games in the final.

Detroit's hopes at slowing the Leafs after Mahovlich was injured were dashed when Eddie Litzenberger had a three-point night subbing for the Big M in Game 2. The series closed with Keon potting the Game 4 winner and adding two short-handed goals at the Gardens in the 3-1 clincher.

It was the first Cup the Leafs had won at the Gardens since the Barilko goal.

TORONTO MAPLE LEAFS
World Champions, Stanley Cup and Prince of Wales Trophy Winners 1962-63

Best of All? The '62-'63 champs were the last Leafs team to finish first in the regular season, winning the final over Detroit in five games. (Hockey Hall of Fame)

1964 CUP

Few believed the Leafs capable of a third con secutive sip from the mug. Imlach's heavy-handed ways were beginning to have an adverse effect as scoring dried up. The Leafs finished third with 192 goals, their worst output in 34 years.

Mahovlich slumped to 26 goals and Imlach grew so impatient with Duff and Nevin that he packaged the duo and Arnie Brown, Rod Seiling and Bill Collins to the Rangers for Andy Bathgate and Don McKenny. He was also on the verge of bringing in a new goaltender.

But the fear factor did the trick. In the opener of the semi-finals, one of the most bloody in the long Leafs-Canadiens rivalry, 31 penalties were called.

Toronto won Game 6 by a 3-0 score, while Keon dominated Game 7 with short-handed, even-strength and empty net goals in a 3-1 victory. The memorable final against Detroit, the NHL's first series to go the distance in nine years, opened at the Gardens in nailbiter fashion.

Toronto

scored short-handed with two seconds left to win, while Detroit took Game 2 on Larry Jeffrey's over-time goal. Game 3 also was settled by last-minute heroics by Alex Delvecchio, while Bathgate and Mahovlich had third-period goals to win Game 4.

Trailing the series 3-2, one of the greatest stories in Leafs lore unfolded when Bobby Baun was struck by a shot in the ankle and taken from the Olympia ice in a stretcher. He came back to score the winner off Bill Gadsby's stick in overtime. It wasn't until after the Leafs were celebrating an easy 4-0 Game 7 win at the Gardens that it was revealed Baun's ankle bone had been fractured.

Baun, Brewer (ribs), Armstrong (separated shoulder) and Kelly (knee) all underwent pre-game injections to fight the pain of injuries, Baun and Kelly going right to the hospital when the game ended. Bower cut himself for six stitches when he tossed his goalstick in the air to celebrate and it came down on his head.

A band leads the way as the Maple Leafs, riding in convertibles, parade on Bay Street.

12

KING CLANCY NIGHT—March 17, 1934

A special tribute game for a sports star was something new to Toronto in the 1930s, but Francis Michael (King) Clancy was the perfect choice for the first such celebration at the Gardens. He'd played every position for the Leafs, including goal.

Though he was just 31 and would play a few more years, Smythe thought it was high time to honor the man who could be called the Leafs' first franchise player.

But the glib Irishman, whom Conn Smythe had acquired from Ottawa through horse racing winnings, was at a loss for words this particular St. Patrick's Day.

"I get a lump in my throat," Clancy said of that evening. "I wasn't a native son, even so they paid me the greatest tribute any hockey player could ever hope to get. I was tongue-tied."

The Leafs were playing the Rangers and Clancy was talked into wearing a green Leafs sweater with a white shamrock on the back. His official introduction by Smythe included telegrams from well-wishers. Several floats with an Irish theme such as a harp, pipe and a potato were brought out, with Leaf teammates hidden inside.

Clancy finally appeared, with a long white beard and a crown, pushed on a makeshift throne by teammate Hap Day. The team presented him with a grandfather clock and a silver tea service for his wife.

Clancy, a three-time all-star, played the first period in his green get-up, but the Rangers demanded he change back to blue and white as he was causing a distraction.

He played until 1937, began a colorful tenure as an NHL on-ice official and was a fixture at Church and Carlton. He filled a number of roles includ-

King for a Day: Clancy enjoys his tribute night, the first ever for a Leaf. (Hockey Hall of Fame)

ing coach of the Leafs from 1953 to '56, never missing the playoffs.

Twice he filled in for ailing Leafs coaches. Many credit his role in the Leafs' last Cup, when he stood in for a sick Punch Imlach for a critical 9-0-1 streak that put them in the playoffs.

He and Harold Ballard became inseparable in the 1970s and '80s, watching the games from the bunker, kibitzing with fans and with each other. On St. Patrick's Day 1975, Metro Chairman Paul Godfrey declared it King Clancy Day in Toronto.

Ballard briefly closed the bunker when Clancy died in 1986 and Clancy lay in state in the directors lounge. Hundreds paid their respects, from Leaf greats to city politicians to the first one in line, the boy who delivered his groceries. When the funeral procession left the church, it drove past the Gardens one last time where the staff gathered out front in salute.

Gardens Events—1938

APRIL 12, Memorial Cup final, St. Boniface 4, Oshawa 0; APRIL 30, pro tennis; MAY 20-21, Dog show; SEPT. 18, Jehovah's Witnesses; OCT. 7, Mann Cup lacrosse final, St. Catharines 18, New Westminster 11; OCT. 8, Paul Whiteman Orchestra; OCT. 24-29, Shrine circus; NOV. 3, 1938-39, home opener, Boston 3, Leafs 2; NOV. 20, Canadian Jewish Congress; NOV. 23, Duke Ellington; DEC. 5-6, Sonja Henie ice show; DEC. 12, Boxing; DEC. 23; Christmas show.

Gardens Events—1939

FEB. 16, wrestling; FEB. 27, boxing; MARCH 6-10, Toronto Skating Club carnival; MARCH 11, tennis; APRIL 10, Memorial Cup final, Oshawa vs. Edmonton; APRIL 20-22, National Electric Show; APRIL 28, IOF pageant; MAY 2, Pro tennis; OCT. 23-28, Shrine circus; NOV. 4, 1939-40, home opener, Boston 5, Leafs 0.

Gardens Events—1940

JAN. 10, Prep school hockey, UCC 10, UTS 1; FEB. 21, Senior city hockey game in aid of Finland; MARCH 4, Boxing; MARCH 18, Ontario Conservative party meeting; APRIL 20, Allan Cup playoffs, Kirkland Lake 8, Calgary 5; OCT. 7, Mann Cup playoffs, Vancouver 14, St. Catharines 9; OCT. 18, Toronto Symphony; OCT. 21-26, circus; NOV. 2, 1940-41, season opener, Rangers 4, Leafs 1; NOV. 8, bingo fund raiser; NOV. 21, Wrestling; DEC. 6, Seaman's Union meeting.

Gardens Events—1941

JAN. 10, wrestling with Whipper Watson; FEB. 13, War Savings youth rally; MARCH 24, War Service Fund meeting; APRIL 21, Memorial Cup opener, Winnipeg 4, Montreal 2; APRIL 25, pro tennis; MAY 10, 48th Highlanders bazaar; MAY 21, Board of Education meeting; MAY 27-31, Buster Crabbe's Water Follies; JUNE 3, Women's Victory Loan Rally; JULY 29, Canadian Corps Association meeting; OCT. 17-18, Toronto Symphony; OCT. 20-25, Shrine circus; OCT. 26, Canadian Tribune lectures; OCT. 27, Cab Calloway; NOV. 1, 1941-42 home opener, Rangers 4, Leafs 3; NOV. 18-21, First Ice Follies show; NOV. 24, boxing; NOV. 29, exhibition hockey, Leafs 8, Brooklyn Americans 2; DEC. 20, Christmas Show.

Gardens Gallery • Dog Meat

Harold Ballard's hound, T.C. Puck, was probably the most famous dog in Gardens history, treated better than some employees and appearing in several team photos in the late 1980s. But the most fearsome canine was a totally unmanagable dog Ballard was given as a present around 1983.

"Harold didn't want it and King Clancy got stuck with it," former general manager Gord Stellick said with a laugh. "It just pulled poor King all over the place. King had to buy a kid a new bicycle because the dog had knocked him right off his old one. This dog howled all night, too."

Except for one evening when Stellick, who was then an assistant, came to the Gardens late one night to finish up some work. He didn't know that Ballard had locked the dog in the executive washroom for a few hours and the beast lunged at him when he answered the call of nature.

"He had me cornered," Stellick recalled. "I don't think I've been more scared."

13

TURK BRODA

While debate will rage about who was the greatest Leafs' forward or defenceman to play at the Gardens in the 20th century, the best goaltenders are a much easier equation.

Terry Sawchuk and Johnny Bower qualify easily, but the most decorated by far was Turk Broda.

Fabulous Fat Man: Broda was ordered to lose weight or lose his job by Conn Smythe in a well-publicized stunt.

He set records for games (629), wins (302) and shutouts (62) that even the long -serving Bower couldn't reach and modern Leafs' workhorse Felix Potvin is barely halfway to challenging.

Broda picked up his first shutout in a 0-0 game at the Gardens against the Montreal Maroons in 1937, his last was a March 3, 1951 home game over Chicago.

In between, the stocky stopper from Brandon, Manitoba, was part of five Stanley Cups, with 13 playoff shutouts, earning him a place in the Hall Of Fame. In the 1949 finals, he allowed just five goals in a four-game sweep of the Red Wings.

His first name was Walter, with the origin of Turk in dispute. It had something to do with either his big freckles, which reminded schoolmates of the spots on turkey eggs, or the way his neck reddened like a turkey's when he got mad.

Whatever, Conn Smythe counted himself lucky the night he was scouting a goalie named Earl Robertson in Detroit and was smitten instead with Broda.

The Wings owned the rights to both and privately laughed when Smythe paid $8000 for the unknown Broda. Always a tad overweight, Broda also helped Smythe in a campaign partly designed to steer publicity away from the football Argonauts.

During the 1949-50 season, Smythe publicaly ordered Broda to lose 10 pounds or be kicked off the team. With the whole city engrossed in the crash diet of "The Fabulous Fat Man", he switched to fruit juice and made it to the required weight at the deadline.

FOSTER HEWITT

He never picked up a shovel or laid a brick, but to millions of Canadians, Foster Hewitt was the man who brought the Gardens to life.

His mere mention of Frank Selke's 10-cent program on the proposed arena back in 1931 brought nearly 100,000 replies and convinced wary investors to join Smythe's enterprise. When Canadian air raid wardens needed binoculars in World War 2, one request from Foster flooded mailboxes.

Smythe knew full well the power of Hewitt and radio and as the Gardens neared completion, he asked Hewitt to choose exactly where he'd like to be positioned for his broadcasts.

Hewitt went to an Eaton's store and kept climbing floor by floor, always keeping an eye on how well he could see the people on the street. He stopped at the fifth and Smythe duly ordered the famous gondola to be hung at 54 feet.

"He made the players into stars," a grateful Red Kelly said.

In the early days, Hewitt and his intermission guests had to negotiate a scary catwalk to reach the gondola, a prospect that so frightened movie tough guy George Raft that he froze and wouldn't cross.

The gondola was in use by Hockey Night In Canada's radio and television arms right up to the late 1970s, when Ballard outraged Hewitt and the Hall Of Fame by trashing it during building renovations. Ballard also grabbed some old chairs,

Hello Hockey Fans . . . Foster Hewitt in the Gondola. (Hockey Hall of Fame)

spraypainted them the same color as Hewitt's favorite gondola seat, stencilled Foster's name on the back and sold a bunch to unsuspecting collectors. But Hewitt's memory could not be cheapened.

"I remember when I was a kid," Don Cherry said. "I'd play road hockey all day long, get into pyjamas, have some cocoa ready and at 9 o'clock, there was Foster."

15

THE WRESTLERS

For a wrestler to appear at the Gardens was like the chance to sing opera at La Scala.

"If you were anyone in wrestling you came to Toronto or St. Louis," said Elio Zarlenga, who worked in publicity for Gardens wrestling in the 1970s, '80s and '90s. "In the early days, Frank and Jack Tunney controlled the big stars in Toronto and Sam Munchnick did the same in St. Louis. But wrestling made it big here primarily because of Frank."

Within a week of the Gardens opening, Tunney's Queensbury Athletic Club card broke an indoor sports record with 15,000 in attendance. In a 75-minute feature match that night, Jim Londos used the aeroplane whirl and body slam to subdue Gino Garibaldi.

In the 1940s, local grappler (Whipper) Billy Watson began a long association with the Gardens and a climb to the world title. Denied in two close decisions to Lou Thesz, one in which the referee was chased by an irate woman brandishing a hat pin, Watson eventully won the title twice.

He also beat the loathsome Gorgeous George for

Gorgeous George—pompous, perfumed and one of the biggest draws in wrestling in his day.

the right to shave the prima donna's blond locks. Watson's charity work on behalf of disabled youngsters was recognized with a Gardens' tribute night on December 17, 1978.

"Whipper was a real crowd favorite," agreed veteran usher Dennis Goodwin. "So were Pat Flanagan and Bulldog Brower in those days. The Sheik was bad, but the guy a lot of people really hated was The Angel. He'd do something outrageous, then run around the ring and the opponent and fans didn't know where he would come out. People went crazy wondering where he was."

Another wrestler who preferred that same escape route under the ring was in for a painful surprise one night. He didn't know workers put a series of steel supports underneath the squared circle for stabilization. When the wrestler dove under and didn't come out, he was eventually found dazed and bleeding.

16

THE MARLBOROS

Toronto couldn't call itself a hockey town without acknowledging the role of Canada's storied junior franchise, the Marlboros.

In many ways, the history of the Leafs parallels the Dukes. A Toronto team went by the name Marlboroughs back as far as 1903, while the junior club was officially formed in 1926, a year before Smythe bought the Leafs.

Original Leafs Charlie Conacher and Busher Jackson were Marlie grads, members of their first Memorial Cup team in 1929. The club won a record seven Cups and sent more than 250 players and coaches on to the NHL, including Leafs Hall of Famers Conacher, Jackson, George Armstrong, Turk Broda and Bob Pulford.

Leaf execs Frank Selke, Harold Ballard, Stafford Smythe and Jim Gregory all got their coaching and

managerial feet wet with the Marlies. The club's last GM was Frank Bonello, now the director of NHL Central Scouting.

"I can still hear Stafford say 'we have to get the people out to watch the Marlies, because they'll be the Leaf fans of tomorrow," Bonello said. "One of the big things was the Saturday junior doubleheaders at the Gardens with St. Michael's (the Marlies' local rivals). We'd play a game at 1 p.m. St. Mike's played at 3 and then the Leafs came on at 8:30. You couldn't beat it for hockey entertainment."

But the Marlies fell into decline in the late 1970s and '80s, with the direct sponsorship of players by the Leafs discontinued with the advent of the universal draft. The rise of the Blue Jays and other forms of entertainment for the young had an effect, as well as lower minor hockey enrollment.

Mighty Dukes: Coach Joe Primeau with two members of his 1948-49 team, defenceman Hugh Bolton (l) and Lorne Pirie (r).

17

ELVIS-April 2, 1957

It was April 2, 1957, when the Gardens turned into Heartbreak Hotel.

Elvis Presley, in his first Canadian appearance, had teenage girls screaming and swooning in their seats. *Toronto Telegram* writer Colin Murray described the two 40-minute performances as "a wavering scream that sank and rose like an air raid siren". Presley often wore earplugs himself on stage, because too much noise caused him to forget words of songs.

Wearing a $2,600 gold laminated suit, Presley caused bedlam with just a wiggle of his thumb or a smile. He accidentally hit himself in the eye with his microphone during the first show at 6 p.m., only to set off more screams.

Presley slipped into town about 3 a.m. the day of the concert, driving his '56 pink Cadillac hardtop with Tennessee plates after a concert in Buffalo. He parked in a Colborne St. garage behind the King Edward Hotel and

checked in under an assumed name. Fans somehow got into the vehicle, making off with cushions, a road map and a valve cap, though 16-year-old Edna Gatherall nearly got away with his driver's registration before being caught.

By the time Presley awoke, a police escort 95-strong was assembling to get him safely to and from the Gardens. District Police Chief George Elliott, admitting he was a fan of The King, nonetheless warned "anyone who gets out of his seat and starts to wander around will be ejected."

But at $3.50 for the top seat, no one was going to cause trouble and the 6 and 9 p.m. shows went off without a hitch. The police did have to restrain a few exuberant girls from rushing the stage, with the help of Elvis's famous manager, Col. Tom Parker. Presley proved very accommodating to Gardens staff during the visit, posing with wrestler Whipper Watson and signing every autograph thrust in front of him.

"A really nice fellow," recalled Gardens public address announcer Paul Morris, who in those days mixed the sound as part of his duties. "Between shows, I pushed him up and down the ramps backstage on one of the equipment carts. He was having a great time."

At the conclusion of the shows many fans ran on stage to collect anything he may have touched, including the dirt on his blue suede shoes. Others charged into the streets hoping to see him leaving. A black Caddy belonging to Metro Chairman Fred Gardiner was mistaken for Presley's and hotly pursued, while the singer got away in a taxi.

The next logical step in a Canadian tour should have been the Montreal Forum, but the Canadiens were unwilling to schedule anything around the Stanley Cup playoffs. Presley never returned to Toronto. Parker objected to high Canadian taxes that ate into their estimated profits of $25,000 to $30,000.

Gardens Events—1942

JAN. 30, Moose Ecclestone tribute; FEB. 12. wrestling; FEB. 18, Gracie Fields; FEB. 23, military hockey tournament; MARCH 2, Victory Loan meeting; MARCH 7, military hockey; APRIL 18, Leafs defeat Red Wings 3-0 to win Cup after losing first three games; APRIL 25, Allan Cup playoffs, Ottawa RCAF 7, Port Arthur 1; MAY 9, Roller Skating Follies; MAY 16, Daughters Of The Empire; MAY 26-30, Water Follies; JUNE 13, Modernaires dance band; JUNE 20, Ned Hamill dance band; JUNE 21, Al St. John Orchestra; JUNE 22-25, Rotary Club convention; JUNE 29, Salute to Canadian army; JULY 2, dance and vaudeville show; JULY 17, Civil Liberties Union meeting; JULY 21, Lion's Club meeting; SEPT. 21, war rally; OCT. 7, Mann Cup playoffs, Mimico-Brampton 10, New Westminster 7; OCT. 13, Citizen's Committee meeting; OCT. 19-24, Shrine Circus; OCT. 26-28, Dionne quintuplets at loan rally; OCT. 29, Leafs raise $10,000 in charity game; OCT. 31, 1942-43, season opener, Leafs 7, Rangers 2; NOV. 17-20, Ice Follies; NOV. 25, Aid To Russia meeting with Wendell Wilkie.

Gardens Events—1943

Feb. 5, Aid To Russia military exhibition game; March 6, Red Cross youth rally; March 8-12, First Ice Capades show; May 3, Victory Loan rally; May 6-8, Roller Follies; May 10, Victory Loan Rally, National War Finance Committee meeting; May 11-12, Sigmund Romberg Orchestra; May 15, 48th Highlanders carnival; June 22, Salute to Russia; Sept. 8, Canadian Jewish Congress; Sept. 12, Guy Lombardo; Oct.11 18-23, Shrine Circus; Oct. 30, 1943-44 home opener, Leafs 5, Rangers 2 (rookie Gus Bodnar scores at record 15-second mark); Nov. 14, war veterans memorial service; Nov. 26, Milk For Britain bingo; Dec. 6-10, Ice Capades; Dec. 31, New Year's Eve dance

Gardens Events—1944

JAN. 8, Babe Pratt's six-assist game vs. Boston; FEB. 18, war savings stamp drive; APRIL 15, Memorial Cup final, Oshawa 9, Trail, B.C., 2 MAY 2-6, Texas Rodeo; MAY 9, Victory Loan rally with Gracie Fields; JUNE 3, 48th Highlanders bazaar; JUNE 23, Canadian - Soviet Friendship meeting; JUNE 26-JULY 1, Garden Bros. circus; SEPT. 20, Bob Hope; SEPT. 25-26, Phil Spitalny's all-girl orchestra; OCT. 1, People's Church meeting; OCT. 7, Mann Cup playoff opener, St. Catharines 17, New Westminster 10; OCT. 8, People's Church meeting; OCT. 10, military lacrosse; OCT. 28, 1944-45 season opener, Leafs 2, Rangers 1; OCT. 30, Andrews Sisters; NOV. 12, Jehovah's Witnesses; NOV. 19, Navy League of Canada; NOV. 27 - DEC. 1, Ice Capades; DEC. 19, Tommy Dorsey Orchestra.

Gardens Gallery • Toughest Tickets

What event in Gardens history created the greatest ticket demand?

A straw poll turned up everything from the building's opening, to Game 7 of the '42 comeback series to the first Beatles' concert to the last game of the '67 playoffs and Game 2 of the Summit Series.

Until the mid 1980s, when every Leaf game sold out, the answer was a difficult one. Lean times for the team cooled the market, except for the annual visit by the Canadiens, until the '93 Leafs put scalpers back on the gravy train.

"In the 1993 playoffs, the number of Gardens seats hadn't gone up, but incomes had risen dramatically from the 1970s," explained one huckster. "That's when you were getting people willing to bid to pay $1,000 a seat."

18

MUHAMMAD ALI-GEORGE CHUVALO FIGHT

This was a battle on three fronts, which would end Conn Smythe's last direct connection to his building.

The reason this heavyweight title fight came to Canada and the Gardens was that Ali, still called Cassius Clay in those days, was considered a traitor in the U.S. He'd denounced the Vietnam war and refused to report for military duty.

No one in the U.S. would sanction Ali's bout with No. 1 challenger Ernie Terrell, so he looked north where the gutsy Chuvalo was climbing the ranks.

Ballard made an offer to host the fight, with the approval of the Gardens' other powerful executives, Stafford Smythe and John Bassett. A strong dissenter was the elder Smythe, whose sense of patriotism couldn't stomach Ali's stance and the thought of him making money in the Gardens as well. Though he'd given up controlling interest in the Gardens to Stafford and his partners in 1961, he made good on a threat to resign as a director and sell his 5,100 minority shares.

The fight took place on March 29, 1966. In the ring, Ali found his Canadian opponent to be 10 times tougher than the "old washer woman" he'd mocked at the prefight press conferences. Through 15 rounds, Chuvalo became the first man Ali failed to knock down in a title fight.

Chuvalo had a kind of home-ring advantage, having fought at the Gardens over 10 years, including a win over Yvon Durelle. Chuvalo had not fared well in his first big pro bouts, losing to Floyd Patterson and Terrell, so few gave him much re-

His Finest Hour: George Chuvalo gives Ali all he can handle at the Gardens.

The Champ: Ali celebrates his hard-earned victory at the Gardens.

spect against Ali. However, 14,000 fans, some of whom paid $100, joined 400 media at the Gardens for the fight.

Ali let Chuvalo and his unrefined punching technique get the better of him in the first rounds, but when Chuvalo didn't tire as the Ali camp hoped, he was forced on the offensive. Chuvalo not only weathered the storm, but gave it right back. Ali won, but only because Chuvalo didn't have the creativity to match his courage.

Telegram writer Bob Pennington called it the best heavyweight bout since Rocky Marciano and Ezzard Charles went the distance 12 years previous.

"He is tougher than Terrell, Patterson or (Sonny) Liston," a more subdued Ali said after the fight. "I hit him with seven or eight good punches, but had to back off, because you just wear yourself out."

Gardens Gallery • Ali Oops

When Muhammad Ali fought George Chuvalo at the Gardens in 1966, he asked for a room to pray to Allah prior to the fight. Not quite grasping what the converted Muslim wanted, Harold Ballard directed him to the nearest washroom. A confused Ali eventually set up in a room near the toilets.

Gardens Gallery • First Gardens Fisticuffs

There wasn't an on-ice official in sight when the first fight in Gardens history took place, in fact there was no ice yet. Witnessed by Conn Smythe and retold in his memoirs 'If You Can't Beat 'Em In The Alley', the brawl was between Cecil Shaw, business agent for the electricians' union and loyal to Smythe, and another member who objected to the idea of taking 20% stock in lieu of payment. "Maybe it was the best fight ever staged at the Gardens," Smythe said. "At the end (Shaw) was on his feet and the other guy was on his back looking up at the sky. The Gardens didn't have a roof at the time."

19

ROCK CROWDS

Stan Obodiac, the late Gardens publicist, estimated that the majority of Torontonians born after 1960 had attended at least one concert at Church and Carlton.

By the mid 1970s, there were almost 50 concerts a year, more than the number of Leafs home games. In the space of a few weeks in the spring of 1976, the diverse schedule included Genesis, Bad Company, Supertramp, Kiss, Frank Sinatra, Paul McCartney, Joe Cocker, Johnny Winter and Santana, all scheduled around the Stanley Cup playoffs.

"Gardens concerts evolved into a cultural event," said *Toronto Sun* entertainment editor Bob

Thompson, who reviewed many rock shows in the 1970s and '80s. "Some didn't even care about the music, they just wanted to take the subway into town, do the walk along Carlton where the scalpers were, then sit around the washrooms and talk, like a high school hangout.

"But for all the crush of people the security

Garden Stones: Mick Jagger and Brian Jones on stage during the 1965 Rolling Stones concert.

Who's at the Gardens?: The so-called "final" show by the Who at the Gardens in December, 1982. (Fred Thornhill/The Toronto Sun)

and the ushers, the scary hair and the clothes, it was really a typical Toronto hockey crowd; they couldn't be polite enough."

Thompson recalls being frightened for his life when he stood up to get a better view of an AC/DC concert he was reviewing and was tapped on the shoulder by an imposing heavy metal rock fan twice his size.

"I thought it was all over for me, but he just said "excuse me sir, I can't see," Thompson recalled with a chuckle.

"You'd get the odd seat torn up and a few fights, but most people behaved."

The more people who attended the concerts, the more sound was absorbed in the building and the less the infamous Gardens sound echo came into play.

"You were usually okay until you got into the high greens and greys," Thompson said. "Then you'd get some sound slaps and lose the lower end of the bass and drums. But all groups who played there suffered through it. The place just wasn't built for modern rock concerts."

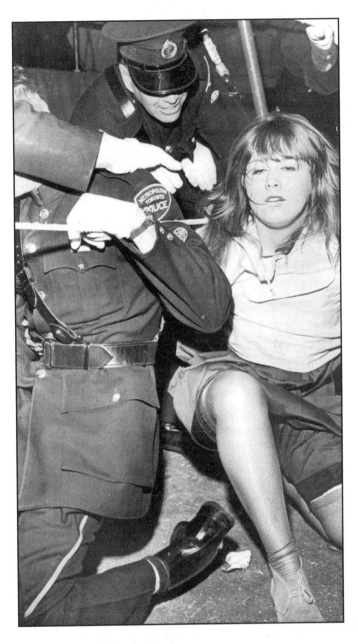

Fans get excited during the Rolling Stones' visit to the Gardens in 1965.

Gardens Gallery •
Sound Advice

The infamous Gardens sound system is hardly a new problem. Within a year of completion, the building crew realized the high ceiling and the tin roof were going to be a headache. An 11-second echo was created when anything on the speaker system hit the roof and bounced back. That led to the hanging of the giant mineral wool batten, some of which is still is place almost 70 years later.

Resembling huge champagne corks, its function is to break up the sound before it gets to the roof. It effectively cut the echo down to six seconds, not perfect, but an improvement.

TEAM CANADA 1972
Game 2, the Summit Series

The only game Team Canada would win on its own soil in the fabled series came at the Gardens, which had been turned over to the NHLers as a training campsite.

The familiarity of the place, after a humiliating 7-3 defeat in Montreal had opened the series two nights earlier, helped Canada get back on its feet.

"I guess I had the players' attention by then," coach Harry Sinden said of the attentive group that surrounded him at centre ice the day after Game 1.

Patriotic signs hung from every corner of the building and the normally staid Toronto audience sang the national anthem loud and proud.

Overwhelmed by the Soviets' speed in Montreal, Sinden changed gears and juggled his lineup for the Toronto game. Tony Esposito went in goal for Ken Dryden, a sixth defenceman was added as the slower Rod Seiling and Don Awrey were dropped in favor of Serge Savard, Bill White and Pat Stapleton.

The entire line of New York Rangers, which was supposed to light up the scoreboard in Montreal, were sacked in favor of the likes of scrappy Stan Mikita, Bill Goldsworthy and Wayne Cashman. The idea was to forecheck harder to negate the Soviet breakout.

After a scoreless first period, big Phil Esposito rewarded the crowd by stealing a puck, changing from backhand to forehand and beating Vladislav Tretiak.

The Soviets' problems with the physical Canadians and their dislike of referee Steve Dowling's work led to a minor penalty to Gynady Tsygankov and a misconduct for an angry Valeri Kharlamov. Yvan Cournoyer made it 2-0 on the power play.

The visitors weren't dead, of course, as Alexander Yakushev scored early in third and a Stapleton penalty caused panic that the Soviets were going to fight off the 2-0 deficit and win. But a brilliant Peter Mahovlich short-handed goal settled the issue, with Frank Mahovlich completing the 4-1 decision.

"That game saved our bacon," Tony Esposito said.

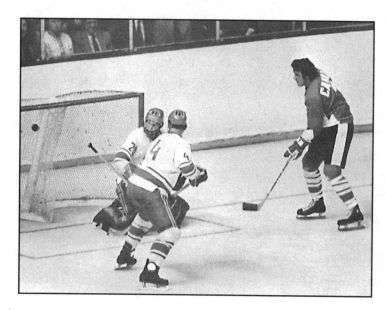

Phil-ling the Net: Canada's Phil Esposito strikes during Game 2 of the '72 Summit Series at the Gardens.

21

CANADA CUP 1976

This tournament was a natural successor to the 1972 series, capitalizing on both the Canada-Russia rivalry and the explosion of hockey in Sweden, Finland, Czechoslovakia and the United States.

For this first high-performance gathering of the clans, the Gardens was to enjoy a lion's share of games. They began on September 3, with Sweden defeating a chippy American side 5-2.

"It's good to be home," Borje Salming noted wryly as the crowd got behind its favorite defenceman and his Tre Kronor teammates. Salming and Leaf teammate Inge Hammarstrom received huge ovations before the game and after, when Salming had a goal and assist and was named first star.

The skate was on the other foot four nights later when Canada played its first Gardens match. Once again, Leafs would play a prominent role, with Darryl Sittler and Lanny McDonald helping linemate Bob Gainey to a two-goal night in a 4-2 win over the Swedes. Bobby Hull and Marcel Dionne had the others.

The last game of the round-robin provided plenty of incentive for Canada, with the Soviets staring at them across the blueline during the national anthems and first place in the tournament on the line.

Team Canada's starting six; Rogie Vachon, Bobby Orr, Serge Savard, Bobby Clarke, Bill Barber

and Reggie Leach, received a standing ovation and 16,485 were on their feet again for the last 20 seconds of the 3-1 victory.

A wild first period saw Canada out-shoot the visitors 18-12, with Gilbert Perreault scoring early and assisting on Hull's eventual game winner. Vladimir Vikulov scored for the Russians.

Vachon and Vladislav Tretiak stole the show from there, Vachon poke checking Helmut Balderis on a breakaway before a Barber goal clinched it.

Game 1 of the best-of-three playoffs saw Canada get a second crack at Czechoslovakian goaltender Vladimir Dzurilla, who had stoned them 1-0 earlier in the tourney. Orr, en route to being named Cup MVP, was a one-man army with seven of Canada's 23 shots, two power-play goals and an assist.

Dzurilla didn't last beyond the first period as Perreault, Denis Potvin, Orr and Guy Lafleur beat him, with Orr and Sittler completing the 6-0 win. Sittler would cap his magical year of '76 a couple of nights later in Montreal, scoring in overtime to win the inaugural Cup.

Czech-Mate: Darryl Sittler is tied up by Bohuslan Ebermann of Czechoslovakia during the 1976 Canada Cup finals. (Barry Gray/The Toronto Sun)

35

22

TERRY SAWCHUK—100TH SHUTOUT

March 4, 1967

To many Leaf fans, he's remembered simply as the winning goaltender the night the club captured its last Stanley Cup.

But Sawchuk was always known for big games in Toronto, from his Calder Trophy win in the 1950-51 season with the Red Wings, to his milestone 100th career shutout on March 4, 1967, 3-0 over Chicago.

A Century of Shutouts: Terry Sawchuk is congratulated for his 100th goose egg. (Hockey Hall of Fame)

But his huge role in the '67 Cup, three previous titles with Detroit and NHL records for games (971) and career shutouts (103) hid many misfortunes for Sawchuk.

His older brother died of a heart ailment, leaving a pair of goal pads that Sawcuk felt compelled to try on even though he might have made it big as a forward.

He suffered some gruesome injuries in the days prior to facial protection, including a stick in the eye in a minor-league game in Omaha. He may have been blinded by the accident, except that a prominent opthamologist happened to be in town that night.

He took an estimated 450 stitches on his face during a career that lasted until 1969-70. In the 1964 playoffs, he came out of hospital after treatment for a pinched nerve in his shoulder to help win a seven-game semifinal for Detroit against the Hawks, only to lose the Cup to the Leafs.

He was in a serious car accident as well. At 39, he had surgery to correct a herniated disc allow-ing him to play three more years.

There might not have been a '67 showdown with Montreal had Sawchuk not withstood the barrage of the fearsome Blackhawks in the six-game semifinal.

After a tough March just to help the underdog Leafs qualify, Sawchuk was outstanding in the first four games. He kept the series at 2-2 against the favored Hawks, who had Bobby Hull, Stan Mikita, and a supporting cast that included Phil Esposito and Ken Wharram.

A battered Sawchuk convinced Punch Imlach to rest him in Game 5, but when Johnny Bower struggled, Sawchuk was inserted again. Hull wounded him right away with shots off the mask and shoulder.

He blocked 22 shots in the final period alone and the Leafs scored four unanswered goals for a 4-2 win. Sawchuk believed he was out of the Montreal series after Bower started so well, but the latter suffered a leg injury in warmup of Game 4 and Sawchuk had to rescue the Leafs again. No Leaf looked more ravaged than Sawchuk in the celebrations following the Cup.

But the team MVP that season was let go to the Los Angeles Kings in the '67 expansion draft.

Rivals such as Bernie Geffrion and Emile Francis called Sawchuk the best goalie ever. But he died from injuries in a playfight with Ron Stewart in May of 1970. He was named to the Hall of Fame the following year.

Gardens Events—1945

FEB. 5-9, Ice Follies; FEB. 16, Toronto Police concert; APRIL 14, Memorial Cup playoffs, St. Michael's 8, Moose Jaw 5; APRIL 30, boxing; MAY 1, Gene Krupa Orchestra; MAY 7-12, Texas Rodeo with Roy Rogers; MAY 23, Tommy Dorsey Orchestra; JUNE 10, United Church meeting; JUNE 15, Charlie Spivak's Orchestra; JUNE 16, Toronto Church youth rally; JUNE 23, Woody Herman Orchestra/Ukrainian festival; SEPT. 11-15, roller skating show; OCT. 5, Tony Pastor Orchestra, OCT. 15-30 Shrine Circus; OCT. 22, Phil Spitalny's all girl Orchestra; OCT. 27, 1945-46 home opener, Leafs 1, Bruins 1; OCT. 30; Victory Loan rally with Fibber McGee and Molly; NOV. 9; women's softball NOV. 21, Canadian - Soviet friendship meeting; NOV. 26-30, Ice Capades; DEC. 31, Ellis McLintock Orchestra.

Gardens Events—1946

JAN. 16; pro and amateur basketball exhibitions; JAN. 29, Toronto Symphony; FEB. 4-8, Ice Follies; FEB. 22, Rotary Club basketball; MARCH 31, Reception for Cardinal McGuigan; APRIL 13, Memorial Cup playoffs, Winnipeg 3, St. Michael's 2; APRIL 25, Teen-Town dance; APRIL 28, Canadian Council of Churches; MAY 1, pro tennis; MAY 3, Drummer's Ball; MAY 7, Board of Education phys ed demonstration; MAY 13-18, Rodeo with Gene Autry; JUNE 14; Canadian - Soviet Friendship meeting; JUNE 15, Youth For Christ rally; JUNE 26, Canadian Legion rally; AUG. 24, Ukrainian concert; SEPT. 10-14, roller skating show; SEPT. 30. Dominion lacrosse final, St. Catharines 11, New Westminster 10; OCT. 9-14, Shrine circus; OCT. 19, 1946-47 home opener, Leafs 6, Detroit 3; OCT. 30, Hadassah Bazaar; NOV. 1, the new NBA plays its first game at the Gardens,New York Knicks 68, Toronto Huskies 66; NOV. 5, Fritz Kreisler concert; NOV. 13, Youth For Christ rally; DEC. 2-6, Ice Capades.

Gardens Gallery • How the Leafs Got Their Name

Within a day of purchasing the Toronto St. Patricks on February 14, 1927, Conn Smythe changed their name to the Maple Leafs, primarily to honor the national emblem on Canadian soldiers' uniforms.

Smythe also had liked the look of the East Toronto Maple Leaves from his amateur scouting days or it may have been that many teams across Canada had used the name or the emblem since the turn of the century. Whatever, he kept the St. Pats green and white design for a year before switching to the now famous blue and white, a likely tribute to his U of T days.

Gardens publicist Stan Obodiac claimed the blue in the Leafs' sweater represented the blue Canadian skies, while the white was the snow, ensuring that ice was always plentiful.

23

FRANK SINATRA—May 10, 1975

When a 59-year-old Frank Sinatra played two Gardens shows (8 p.m. and midnight) more than 36,000 attended, a building record for one man in one day. He generated both money—a $500,000 gross—and a little controversy, stopping his act to hold up a *Toronto Star* and deny its story that his bodyguard had slugged the paper's photographer.

But fans who'd waited for years for Ol' Blue Eyes to play the Gardens were richly rewarded. During his 15 songs, he also displayed a "good luck" card given to him by the building staff and didn't get riled during *My Way* when a heckler shouted "don't you ever quit?".

But when another yelled "I love you Frank", there were loud cheers. Sun music critic Wilder Penfield III remarked that Sinatra's voice was showing its age, but professionalism and skillful vocal theatrics got him through any rough spots.

He played the Gardens a year later and once more attracted sellout crowds. Sinatra was given the Leafs dressing room as his quarters, a rare honor, which was well stocked with Jack Daniel's and baskets of fruit for him to nibble between shows.

Blue Eyes in the Gardens: Frank Sinatra in his 1975 Gardens appearance. (Barry Gray/Toronto Sun)

24

FIRST NBA GAME

You think of the Gardens as the hotbed of hockey, not the cradle of the National Basketball Association.

But the first game in league history took place here on November 1, 1946, when the New York Knickerbockers out-dueled the Toronto Huskies 68-66 before a crowd of 7,000.

In a special promotion, anyone taller than Toronto's 6-foot-8 centre George Nostrand was admitted free. Knicks' Ossie Schectman recorded the league's first field goal on a layup bounce from Leo Gottlieb, Ed Sadowski of the Huskies led all scorers with 18 points.

The Huskies pushed hard to get a big-name Canadian on their roster, adding Argo great Joe Krol's name to the opening night program in hopes he'd accept their offer to play. They settled for Hank Biasatti and Gino Sorvan, both of Windsor.

Biasatti went in for Charlie Hoefer with 30 seconds to play and a chance to win the game, but the Tely's game story noted "his anxiousness ruined the play and one almost sure chance was blown."

Biasatti, who made $600 a month as a Huskie, went on to play three years of major league baseball for the

Philadelphia Athletics after being drafted from the baseball Maple Leafs.

The NBA was called the Basketball Association of America then and hoop hopes were high that the Toronto market would be as successful as hockey at the Gardens. But the Huskies, who wore blue and white tops in deference to the Leafs, ended up tied with the Boston Celtics for last place.

"The fans just weren't ready for basketball," Biasatti told the *Toronto Sun* in 1993. "There's no way it could compete with hockey. But there's a big difference between then and now."

He was refering to the arrival of the Toronto Raptors that year. In several appearances at the Gardens in their first three seasons, the Raptors drew good crowds and players and fans declared it much more intimate than their SkyDome headquarters.

The NBA had made sporadic visits after the Huskies, such as Wilt Chamberlain, Elgin Baylor, Jerry West and the Lakers coming in for a game in 1971 against the Cincinnati Royals. The Buffalo Braves played a series of home games in the early 1970s, but talk of moving that franchise here never came to pass.

Tip Off: The first NBA game at the Gardens. (City of Toronto Archives)

25

DOUG GILMOUR IN '93 PLAYOFFS

Forty-eight hours earlier the Leafs had set the town on its ear with a dramatic seventh-game overtime goal to upset Detroit in the first round of the 1993 playoffs. Now the Leafs were locked in the 84th minute of a 1-1 game against the well rested St. Louis Blues.

Once again, they turned to their captain, Doug (Killer) Gilmour, who had rallied them points in the deciding game at Joe Louis Arena and was drawing on every fuel reserve in his emaciated body.

Gilmour found himself with the puck behind Curtis Joseph, a Leaf nemesis, who'd already faced 63 shots, a 35-year Leafs playoff high. Dancing later-

ally at a furious pace to each side of the net to work Joseph and the Blues defence out of position, Gilmour finally went for the right-side wraparound and found the tiny hole he needed. The building exploded, as the clock neared midnight.

"That's the longest game I've ever played in," Gilmour said with a sigh later. "I couldn't decide what side to come out of. I'd still be there if I hadn't finally (acted)."

Toronto eventually would triumph 6-0 at the Gardens in the seventh game of the series, claiming the last Norris Division playoff title before the league changed to a conference format in post season the following year.

Killer instinct: Doug Gilmour stuffs the puck under Blues goalie Curtis Joseph, a future Leaf, to give the Leafs a 2-1 double overtime victory at the Gardens. (Craig Robertson/The Toronto Sun)

26

1945 CUP

As the war wound down, the Leafs got Nick Metz, John McCreedy and Wally Stanowski out of military uniforms and back into blue and white sweaters. Smythe returned from Europe as well, his 30th Sportsmen's battery of athletes, Gardens employees and writers having distinguished themselves.

There would be plenty of excitement for them on the home front, with the Leafs beating the Habs in a six-game semi-final, despite Rocket Richard being at the height of his scoring prowess.

Calder winner Frank McCool, whose surname belied a nervous character, stunned the Red Wings with three straight shutouts, 1-0, 2-0, 1-0 to open the series. Detroit, with future Leaf Harry Lumley in goal, then threatened to match the Leafs' heroics from '42 by winning the next three, including the last ever 1-0 overtime Leafs loss in the Gardens.

Babe Pratt came to the rescue with 7:46 to play in Game 7, breaking a 1-1 tie to clinch the Cup.

Signatures of the 1944-45 Cup Winners.

Gardens Gallery • VIPs

Here's a partial list of VIPs who've presided at the ceremonial opening faceoffs covering 67 years of the Leafs: Princess Elizabeth, Marilyn Bell, Hap Day, Louis St. Laurent, Conn Smythe, Lester Pearson, John Diefenbaker, Toronto Mayor William Stewart, Dieppe veterans, Victoria Cross winners, Frederick Gardiner, Premier George Drew, Premier John Robarts, Premier Bill Davis, Clarence Campbell, King Clancy, Swedish ambassador Ake Malmaeus, Gordon Sinclair, Ben Johnson, Robert Stanfield, Governor General Lord Alexander, Lieutenant Governor Pauline McGibbon, Joe Primeau, Whipper Watson, Cardinal Carter and Police Chief Harold Adamson.

27

1947 CUP

From the ashes of missing the playoffs for the first time since the Gardens went up, the Leafs righted their ship in short order and won four Cups in the next five years.

McCool had quit, Pratt was disciplined for gambling, and another casualty was Frank Selke, who left to join the Canadiens prior to the season, having done so much for the Gardens' formative years.

Once more, a championship would coincide with a Calder Trophy as Howie Meeker fired 27 goals, one of six new faces on the youngest team ever to win a Cup to then.

The strength of the team could be found in the likes of Ted (Teeder) Kennedy, who was pressed into the Leafs lineup during the war years and now led them in every offensive category. Kennedy was later to recall this team was full of wounded or returning war vets, anxious minor leaguers and dissatisfied Leafs from the season before, all spoiling to prove to Smyth and coach Hap Day that they hadn't lost a step.

Captain Syl Apps, who had five goals in the playoffs, centred Meeker and Vic Lynn in the league's first all-Canadian final in 12 years.

Toronto rebounded from a 6-0 opening-game loss to Montreal, after which the Leafs made Hab goalie Bill Durnan eat his words about Toronto being a fluke playoff team. Kennedy scored the 2-1 winner late in Game 6 at the Gardens.

The Champions: The Leafs pose with the 1947 Cup, the first of three straight. (Hockey Hall of Fame)

28

1948 CUP

The departing Apps had been the last NHL-captain to cart away a cigar-shaped Stanley Cup and now became the first to pose with the new ringed model.

More new faces were to surround him in the victorious title picture after a seven-player trade Smythe pulled early in the year. Smythe badly wanted Max Bentley, swift centre on Chicago's famed Pony Line. It cost him Bob Goldham, Ernie Dickens, Bud Poile, Gaye Stewart and Gus Bodnar to get Bentley and Cy Thomas, but the dividends were immense.

The Leafs became a three-line threat, anchored by Apps, Kennedy and Bentley, ready to take on the great Production Line in Detroit, which loomed as a championship matchup.

Bentley delivered 48 points in his first 53 games, while the Leafs lost just one playoff game and held the Production Line to a Ted Lindsay goal. Gordie Howe was blanked in his Cup debut.

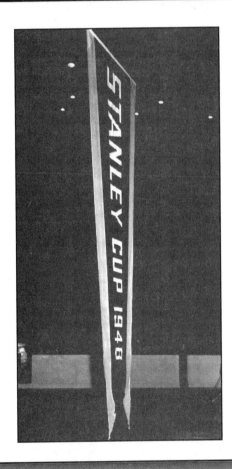

Banner Season: The Leafs' 1948 Cup Banner, the second of three straight, is raised to the roof. (Hockey Hall of Fame)

Gardens Gallery • Seating Capacity

This chart shows how the Gardens' seating capacity changed through the years, with standing room: 1931-40 12,473; 1947-60 12,586 (14,550); 1962-64 13,718 (14,650); 1966-67 15,461 (16,161); 1971-76 16,316 (16,485); 1982-91 16,182 (16,382); 1995-98 15,646 (15,746)

29

1949 CUP

Apps and Nick Metz were retired, the Leafs appeared to be running out of steam, but Smythe made another provocative trade, getting centre Cal Gardner and defenceman Bill Judza from the Rangers. Meanwhile, the seeds Smythe had sown three years earlier with a youth movement saw Jim Thomson, Gus Mortson, Bill Barilko and Frank Mathers all contribute.

In the final, however, it would be unheralded Leafs such as Ray Timgren, Sid Smith and Joe Klukay scoring big goals to support Broda. Smith had the hat trick in Game 2 in a 3-1 win and once more, Howe, Abel and Delvecchio ground to a halt in a four-game sweep.

The Leafs became the first NHL team to win three straight Cups since the days of the Ottawa Silver Seven. Bentley, who no longer thought about the car the Hawks were going to buy him had he stayed and won the '46-47 scoring title, told author Brian McFarlane: "I didn't know anything about winning until I came to the Leafs.

"Day was strict, but he was smart and he knew the game. With Day, there was no monkey business in practice. I believe the way you practice is the way you play."

Teeder Makes Three: In his first year as Leafs' captain, Ted "Teeder" Kennedy celebrates Toronto's third consecutive Cup in 1949. The new-look Cup had a twist-off top. (Hockey Hall of Fame)

30

TIM HORTON

At the Leafs' 1951 training camp, the mourning for Bill Barilko eventually gave way to optimism that another strapping lad from Northern Ontario could one day replace the missing hero.

Tim Horton did indeed become a mainstay on the blue line, with a Leafs' career that spanned three decades. When he took to the Gardens ice on February 11, 1961, a 6-3 win over Boston, he would begin a string of 486 consecutive games, still a club record.

The run ended late in the 1967-68 season, by which time Horton had helped the Leafs to four Stanley Cups. The man in the same team picture as Barilko was around long enough to break in Brian Glennie as a defence partner.

Horton's strength was legendary, with even the robust Gordie Howe praising his power. He would often grab two opponents during a fight in the famous Horton Hug and didn't flinch when a team doctor reset a broken leg during a game that would've had others in agony.

Horton was a six-time all-star, was the first Leaf to play in 1,000 games and was clearly the best Toronto defenceman ever in the minds of those who grew up in the Original Six days. In the 1962 playoffs, the first of three straight Cups, he set a record with 12 assists in 13 playoff games.

He was traded to the Rangers on March 3, 1970, for Guy Trottier, Denis Dupere and Jacques Plante, eventually finding his way to Buffalo to be reunited with Punch Imlach. The 1973-74 season was going to be his last as he prepared to run a chain of doughnut stores bearing his name.

But in the early morning hours of February 21, 1974, following a 4-2 loss to the Leafs, Horton's sports car crashed en route back to Buffalo. He was dead at 44.

Big Blue Wrecking Crew: Tim Horton is considered by many to be the Leafs' greatest defenceman. (Hockey Hall of Fame)

31

THE BIG M: FRANK MAHOVLICH

Darryl Sittler holds the club's career scoring records, but it was Frank Mahovlich who received the most votes of any Leaf forward when a *Hockey News* panel chose the top 50 players in history. The Big M was 26th, with only Terry Sawchuk and Red Kelly ahead of him among ex-Leafs.

The intimidating left winger had no troubles with hockey so long as his focus was 200 X 85 feet. Nine all-star selections and nearly a point a game in more than 1,181 starts is clear proof.

"Bobby Hull may score more goals," teammate

Big M in Flight: Frank Mahovlich scores against Montreal.

Dave Keon said, "but no one scores better goals than Frank."

But outside pressures ate away at the Timmins native, who was brought south and enrolled at St. Michael's. His quest for 50 goals in 1960-61 petered out two goals short and constant arguing with Imlach dulled his edge.

Chicago nearly paid the Leafs $1 million for Mahovlich after a late night party, but the deal was killed in the sober light of day. In Detroit, and later Montreal, Mahovlich broke the defensive shackles Imlach had him wear.

Gardens Events—1947

JAN. 8, Rookie Howie Meeker's five-goal game; FEB. 3-7, Ice Follies; FEB. 24, Alex Templeton Show; MARCH 23, Crippled Children's benefit; APRIL 19, Leafs beat Montreal 2-1 to win their fourth Cup; APRIL 29-30, Ice Revue with Barbara Ann Scott; MAY 2, Kiwanis Club Male Chorus; MAY 9, Drummer's Ball; MAY 15, wrestling; JUNE 23, boxing; AUG. 18-19, Roman choir; SEPT. 18, wrestling; SEPT. 23-27, roller skating show; OCT. 6-11, Shrine circus; OCT. 13, NHL all-stars beat the Leafs 4-3; OCT. 18, 1947-48 season opener, Leafs 2, Detroit 2; OCT. 19, Crippled Children's benefit; OCT. 20, Teen-Town dance; OCT. 28, Hadassah Bazaar; NOV. 17-20, Ice Capades.

32

HOCKEY NIGHT IN CANADA

John Shannon calls a Hockey Night In Canada broadcast from the Gardens "classic Canadian theatre".

"It's hockey and fantasy mixed together," said HNIC's executive producer. "Television just makes the Gardens look so huge to the viewer. The blue seats seem bluer, the reds look redder. You see those tight corners, the bars around the gold rail seats ... that's the Gardens signature.

"When you take somebody who has watched the Leafs for years on TV and show them the actual rink and our studio, they're shocked, they wonder 'is that all there is?'. It does look so much bigger on TV."

The spartan studio, where more than 2,100 player interviews have taken place and where Don Cherry booms out Coach's Corner with Ron MacLean is actually just a few feet away from the

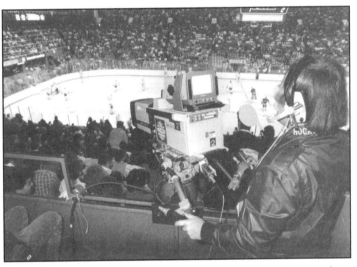

Hockey Theatre: Hockey Night in Canada and the Gardens share a rich history. (Greig Reekie/Toronto Sun)

Leafs dressing room. Team benches and the ice are just a few steps the other way, a nicely compact arrangement.

"What happens in the studio is a microcosm of the Gardens," Shannon said. "It's not fancy, it doesn't have huge balconies and you can walk around at ice level. One of the really great things is that when the little guy in Row D has to go to the bathroom, you see him get up and step right behind the players and coaches to get by with no glass in between them. That simplicity is missing just about everywhere else."

Hockey Night, the nation's No. 1 sports show, requires 14 cameras, nine operators and a total of about 45 technicians on an average Saturday night. The bill usually comes to around $125,000 Cdn..

Fewer resources are needed for the mid-week telecasts, but the rarely seen nerve centre for both shows are the mobile trucks parked behind the Gardens on Wood St.

33

DARRYL SITTLER'S FIVE-GOAL PLAYOFF GAME

In a playoff series that might have been the dirtiest and most controversial in club history, Darryl Sittler brought a touch of class.

Game 6 of this quarter-final against the Flyers could have been a black mark on the Gardens and hockey, remembered only for the 185 penalty minutes, a record up to then. But the story was Sittler's five-goal game in the 8-5 victory.

No Leaf did that in post-season before or since and only five have managed it in NHL playoff history. As was the case with his record 10-point night the same year, Sittler was in a slump, with no goals in eight games and his team facing elimination.

It had been a violent series even by the Broad St. Bullies' standards, with incidents on and off the ice and Ontario Attorney General Roy McMurtry pondering legal action against the visitors.

Sittler lifted the cloud with a second-period hat trick, on a night that would include two goals within 32 seconds. He beat Bernie Parent with a low power-play drive, knocked in an Errol Thompson rebound and scored as Joe Watson hauled him down on a rush.

Sittler batted another in from Parent's glove after the latter couldn't squeeze a George Ferguson rebound.

"It was another lucky night," Sittler said, though he tried to give fate a push by putting his sticks under one of coach Red Kelly's pyramids. Kelly thought the mystic symbols would give the Leafs a power surge and Sittler's endorsement led to Leaf fans making their own pyramids for Game 7. But the Flyers won and carried the series.

Take Five: One of Darryl Sittler's five goals in one playoff game on Philadelphia's Bernie Parent in 1976. (Hugh Wesley/Toronto Sun)

34

BORJE SALMING

War in the Middle East, a disgraced Spiro Agnew and Harold Ballard's imminent parole dominated the headlines on October 10, 1973. It was the night a lanky Swede took to the ice for the first time in a Leafs sweater, played a strong game and assisted on a Sittler goal in a 7-4 win over Buffalo.

Just off the boat from Kiruna, a mining post were his grandfather herded reindeer, Salming had to communicate in hand gestures. When he was named one of the three stars, he had to be shown how to go out and take a bow.

Playing 1,098 more games with the Leafs was probably the last thing on his mind that night, but he would become one of just five Leafs to reach such a milestone.

He was to become the greatest scoring defenceman in club history, but will be forever remembered around the league as the pioneer whom Swedish players would follow the next 25 years.

"Every Swede who draws an NHL salary should send a portion to Borje Salming," broadcaster Harry Neale said in 1997.

"He broke the color barrier in hockey."

Fans took an immediate liking to the Viking and his batch of head fakes and stick schnooks. Salming was a first or second-team all-star six times.

Salming won over the Leafs through his bravery in the face of NHL ruffians. who targeted this so-called "chicken Swede". In his second game, Salming was given an awful beating by the Flyers' Dave Schultz.

Honesty about an earlier experiment with drugs brought him an eight-game suspension in the late 1980s, but plenty of public support. He played in the NHL until 1989, and in Sweden, until he was 40. He survived a 200-stitch cut in a game in Detroit after getting stomped on by a skate in a goalmouth pileup. His 620 assists will stand many more years as the club record.

Salming takes out Pittsburgh's Pat Hughes in 1980. (above) Swede Seasons: Borje Salming was a fan favorite and got along with Harold Ballard's dog, team mascot, T.C. Puck. (Tim McKenna/ The Toronto Sun)

35

CONCERTS IN THE '60s AND '70s

The Gardens' reign as Canada's premier rock venue dates from 1956-57 when Bill Haley and the Comets brought Rock Around The Clock to town and Elvis took the city by storm.

In 1962, Chubby Checker not only had 'em twisting in the aisles, but, according to Stan Obodiac, he became the first Gardens performer to borrow a Leafs' sweater and wear it on stage. It was noted Checker never returned the jersey, but a tradition was begun, embraced by such stars as Roger Daltry of The Who, Elton John and the members of Abba.

The first of three annual visits by the Beatles in 1964 raised sound levels to new heights, as did the Rolling Stones' first show in 1965. Johnny Cash, the first country music star to make it big at the Gardens, broke attendance records with more than 18,000 watching his 1969 show.

But fans, not musicians were making most of the racket. In the spring of 1969, with power guitars now the norm, groups such as the Jimi Hendrix Experience began bringing their own heavy duty equipment to overcome the effects of the cavernous Gardens.

Concert notables— Rolling Stones (4/25/65); Beach Boys (9/5/65); Beatles (8/17/66); Monkees (4/2/67); James Brown (11/15/68); Doors (3/21/69); Jimi Hendrix (5/3/69).

Fats Domino was one of many performers to appear at the Gardens in the '50s and '60s. (City of Toronto Archives)

36

WRESTLING'S TRUE-TO-LIFE MOMENTS

Convinced he was illegaly pinned by Jim Londos in a 1939 bout, Joe Savoldi sat in the middle of the ring as a protest. He was still there hours later when workers began converting for a Leafs game and the ring literally was torn down around him when he finally stalked off.

As the hated Killer Kowalski strutted off after winning an unpopular decision in the 1950s, an irate man, about half the grappler's size, jumped on the ramp and smacked him. Kowalski, wearing his trunks and wrestling boots, chased the guy around the building, out the North West exit and down Wood St. All evil wrestlers who en-

tered and left could expect a whack on the head from the umbrella of an elderly woman who sat above the runway. A well-to-do older woman had her chauffeur not only drive her to the Gardens, but stand by with a blanket and other creature comforts as she hollered away to her heart's content. During a 1980s bout between Andre the Giant and King Kong Bundy, the Giant was actually knocked cold. About 10 wrestlers came out to try to lift the Giant on a gurney, which snapped under his several hundred pounds, while some in the crowd howled with laughter believing it was part of the show.

1965 wrestling hero Johnny Valentine looks bad and bloody as the villain of the wrestling ring, Bulldog Brower, applies a head-shrinking hold.

37

ICE FOLLIES/CAPADES

At one time, the Leafs never surrendered a Saturday night at the Gardens for any rival event. That changed in a hurry as shows such as the Ice Follies and Ice Capades began selling out. The Gardens was tailor-made for the huge skating spectacles that were booked within a few years of its opening.

Local groups, such as the Toronto Skating Club, beat the big shows to the Gardens by staging wonderful costumed specials in the mid-1930s. Then came Hollywood star Sonja Henie, who drew 12,000 just before Christmas 1938, though the crowd was just as anxious to see her partner, local boy Stewart Reburn.

Shipstad's and Johnson's Ice Follies began a long and successful association with the Gardens as far back as 1941. The talented Swiss clown Mr. Frick was in the first show and was still delighting audiences four decades later.

Two years after the Follies debut, the Ice Capades, another American production, came to Toronto and earned a loyal following as well.

Anytime famous Canadian skaters such as Barbara Ann Scott, Donald Jackson, Lynn Nightingale and Otto and Maria Jelinek were part of either a show or their own revue, the crowd would be even more responsive.

The tradition continued into the 1970s, 80s

Ice shows have been a Gardens tradition since the 1930s.

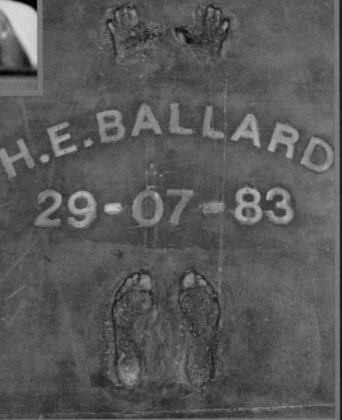

Harold Ballard in his bunker in 1988. (Veronica Milne/Toronto Sun)

When a new Garden floor was installed in 1983, Harold Ballard left his signature at center ice. (Ken Kerr/Toronto Sun)

H.E. BALLARD

29-07-83

 Roger Neilson guided the Leafs as coach from 1977-79. (Canada Wide Photo)

John Brophy (above) was behind the Leafs bench from 1986-88. (Bill Sandford/Toronto Sun)

 With the arrival of Cliff Fletcher (right) as president in 1991 and the hiring of Pat Burns as coach, the Leafs embarked on their best years since 1967. (Canada Wide Photo)

Frank Mahovolich battles the Bruins. (Tim McKenna/ Toronto Sun)

Wendel Clark and Darryl Sittler at a press conference to announce Clark was getting the 'C'. (Tim McKenna/ Toronto Sun)

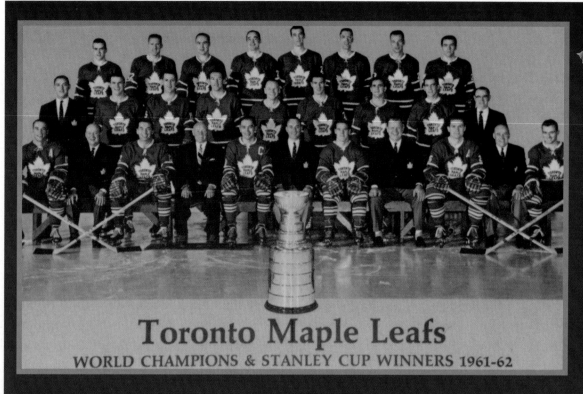

Toronto Maple Leafs
WORLD CHAMPIONS & STANLEY CUP WINNERS 1961-62

The 1961-62 World Champions.

The Toronto Maple Leafs' 1966-67 champs.

World Champions and Stanley Cup Winners 1966/67

FRONT ROW, left to right: George "Punch" Imlach (Manager and Coach), George Armstrong (Captain), John Bassett (Chairman of the Board), C. Stafford Smythe (President), Harold E. Ballard (Executive Vice-President), Bob Pulford, Frank "King" Clancy (Assistant Manager-Coach). SECOND ROW, left to right: Johnny Bower, Dave Keon, Larry Hillman,

Red Kelly, Frank Mahovlich, Tim Horton, Bob Baun, Terry Sawchuk. THIRD ROW, left to right: Ron Ellis, Marcel Pronovost, Peter Stemkowski, Allan Stanley, Eddie Shack, Larry Jeffrey, Mike Walton. FOURTH ROW, left to right: Bob Haggert (Trainer), Milan Marcetta, Brian Conacher, Jim Pappin, Aut Erickson, Tom Nayler (Assistant Trainer).

MAPLE LEAF GARDENS

Marlies' Glenn Lowes (left) and North Bay's Troy Crowder slug it out at the Gardens. (Paul Henry/Toronto Sun)

Peterboro's Mike Ricci in Ontario Hockey League action at the Gardens. (Toronto Sun)

Toronto Marlboro's Mike Jackson raises his arms in jubilation after scoring against Cornwall. (Craig Robertson/Toronto Sun)

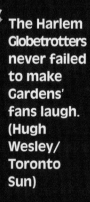

George
Chuvalo
(right) gives
Muhammad
Ali all he can
handle.
(Toronto Sun)

The Harlem
Globetrotters
never failed
to make
Gardens'
fans laugh.
(Hugh
Wesley/
Toronto
Sun)

 Ice shows have been a Gardens tradition since the 1930s. (Ken Kerr/Toronto Sun)

 Terry Head, clown prince of skating comedy. (Ken Kerr/ Toronto Sun)

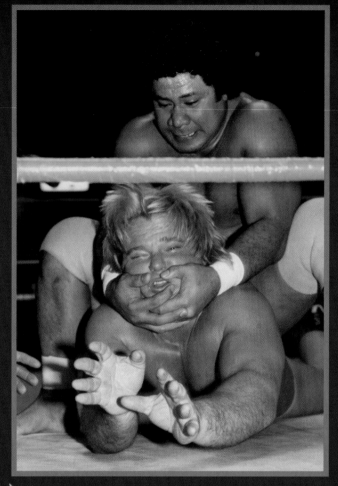

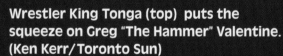
Wrestler King Tonga (top) puts the squeeze on Greg "The Hammer" Valentine. (Ken Kerr/Toronto Sun)

The Blue Blazer gets into some heavy head twisting action on whipping-boy Steve Lombardi. (Tim McKenna/Toronto Sun)

Devoted wrestling fans get worked up into an instant lather over the bad and good guys. (Norm Betts/Toronto Sun)

 Prince turns the Gardens purple in 1984. (Dimo Safari/ Toronto Sun)

 Neil Young rocks on for a full house in Maple Leaf Gardens in 1991. (Mark O'Neill/Toronto Sun)

 Every Leafs game was sold out from opening night in 1931 until late in the 1980s. (Toronto Sun)

 Gardens employees Brian Woodhouse (left) and Tony DeAngelis are all smiles after helping clean the ice. (Mike Peake/Toronto Sun)

 Maple Leaf Gardens' usherettes, having completed their appointed rounds of directing gold-ticket holders to their seats, chat it up while the game goes on. (Mike Peake/Toronto Sun)

 Organist Brian Larter peeks out at the proceedings on the ice from his perch high in the southeast corner of the Gardens. (Mike Peake/Toronto Sun)

 The original Gardens safe was so bulky that renovations were carried on around it. (Mike Cassese/ Toronto Sun)

An old spiral staircase was kept intact after renovations to the Gardens in the 1990s. (Mike Cassese/ Toronto Sun)

 A janitor mops up as another night of hockey draws to a close at Maple Leaf Gardens. (Mike Peake/ Toronto Sun)

and 90s, with Toronto's Toller Cranston part of the World Figure Skating Tour. He eventually started his own company in the late '70s, an idea developed further in the 1990s by Elvis Stojko's Tour of Champions.

The world champion Canadian team of Paul Martini and Barbara Underhill gave a special performance in May of 1998 to mark their retirement.

King Clancy and an ice dancer pose for a publicity shot. (Hockey Hall of Fame)

Garden Events—1948

JAN. 5, boxing; JAN. 21, Detroit Symphony; FEB. 2-6, Ice Follies; FEB. 19, wrestling; MARCH 21, Crippled Children's benefit; MAY 10-11, Olympic team basketball tryouts; MAY 14-15, Phil Spitalny's all-girl Orchestra; MAY 16, Zionist meeting; JUNE 15-19, Aqua Parade; OCT. 4-9, Shrine circus; OCT. 11, Mann Cup final, New Westminster def. Hamilton; OCT. 16, 1948-49 home opener,Boston 4, Leafs 1; OCT. 22, Teen-Town dance; NOV. 2, Hadassah Bazaar; NOV. 8-12, Ice Capades.

Garden Events—1949

JAN. 31-FEB. 4, Ice Follies; FEB. 16, Toronto police concert; MARCH 3, wrestling; APRIL 3, Crippled Children's benefit; APRIL 16, Leafs beat Detroit 3-1 to win third straight Cup;MAY 4, Allan Cup final, Ottawa defeats Regina; MAY 10-14, Ice Revue; MAY 15, military bands; JUNE 21, Liberal party rally; AUG. 8-11, Order of the Eastern Star parade; AUG. 18-19, Miss Canada pageant; SEPT. 19, boxing; OCT. 3-8, Shrine circus; OCT. 10, NHL all-stars beat Leafs 3-1;OCT. 12, Bob Hope; OCT. 15, 1949-50 home opener, Leafs 4, Black Hawks 3; NOV. 7-11, Ice Capades.

Gardens Events—1950

JAN. 23, boxing; JAN. 30 - FEB. 3, Ice Follies; Feb. 21, Toronto police concert; March 20, boxing; MARCH 27, Order of the Eastern Star parade; APRIL 2, Crippled Children's benefit; April 29, Memorial Cup final, Montreal defeats Regina; May 7, Canadian Slavic Committee meeting; MAY 15, Spike Jones; MAY 23, Shrine convention; MAY 26, Manitoba Flood Relief Fund meeting; MAY 31, Jack Benny; JUNE 11, United Church meeting; Aug. 14, Canadian Council of Churches; OCT. 1-7, Shrine circus; Mann Cup final, New Westminster defeats Owen Sound; OCT. 14, 1950-51 home opener, Chicago 2, Leafs 1; NOV. 7, Horcae Heidt Orchestra; NOV. 13-17, Ice Capades.

Gardens Gallery • Going Up?

The Gardens was the first indoor arena in North America to have escalators to get fans to the upper reaches of the arena.

Unfortunately, it took the better part of the 1955-56 season to install them, longer than the 5½ months needed to build the entire Gardens in 1931. Conn Smythe lorded that over his staff for years.

38

ROYALTY AT THE GARDENS

Whenever the British royal family is in town, it seems right at home at the Gardens.

On October 13, 1951, a year before her coronation, Princess Elizabeth and Prince Phillip were present to watch a special 3 p.m. exhibition between the Leafs and Blackhawks, who played the full season opener later that night.

The future Queen was presented with a game puck by Conn Smythe, who informed her he was putting her young son Charles on the Leafs negotiating list. On the night of the Gardens' 50th anniversary, November 12, 1981, the Queen sent a congratulatory telegram to the Gardens.

A teenaged Prince Andrew visited the Leafs dressing room between periods of a game against Buffalo in 1977 and was amused when Tiger Williams shouted "Hi Andy!" as he entered. Andrew made a couple of other visits while attending a private school near Toronto, but he wore disguises as he attended rock shows.

Smythe naturally had deep respect for the Royals. The Queen's portrait hung at the south end for years, until Harold Ballard had it removed for more seats.

Two of the three Leaf games ever cancelled in Gardens history were in 1936 and '52 when King George V and King George VI died.

Game Cancelled: The only time a Leafs game has been postponed was the death of a British monarch, in this case, George VI in 1952.

The memorial service at the Gardens for King George V in 1936.

39

COLORFUL LEAFS

The sixties were a golden age of music, but the hot record in Toronto for awhile had nothing to do with the Beatles or Rolling Stones. The upbeat tune went something like:

Clear the track, here comes Shack
He knocks them down and he gives 'em a
whack
He can score goals, he's found the knack,
Eddie, Eddie Shack.

No. 23 caused mayhem on the ice and off, gabbing on the bench, taunting the enemy, starting fights and then leading with his famous nose instead of a right hook. He could score as well, 20 goal-seasons with five different teams.

The Entertainer often led the Gardens in his own chant of "We want Shack" and charged out for three-star bows like an old Olympic barrel-jumper.

But comedians and free spirits have been living a double life as Leafs since the first dressing room pranks in 1931. King Clancy would cavort in a green sweater, Babe Pratt would stay out late and charm his

The Entertainer: Eddie Shack in action. (Hockey Hall of Fame)

way down Carlton St. to work in the morning, or Carl Brewer would drive Punch Imlach nuts by beating him at his own head game.

Bill Barilko and Turk Broda gave way to Shack, Jim McKenny and then Tiger Williams, the club's career penalty king, who brought down a grizzly with a bow and arrow and presented its carcass to Harold Ballard. Williams had the best post-goal act in team history, riding his stick like a bronco or touching the Tiger-Cat logos Ballard put on the Gardens ice when he owned Hamilton's CFL team.

The late John Kordic walked too far on the wild side, while the mid-90s Leafs were successful in part because they were so loose; led by Mike Foligno, Glenn Anderson, Ken Baumgartner and Todd Gill.

Goaltenders are a breed apart to start, but the Leafs have had a fair share of eccentrics. There were nervous nellies such as Frank (Ulcers) McCool, roly-poly Broda, Jacques Plante knitting toques, Mike Palmateer gobbling Gardens' popcorn and Felix Potvin, painted head to toe like a cat and playing punk rock to unwind after games.

GREAT BOXING MATCHES

Boxing never failed to draw a crowd to the Gardens, whether it was a local amateur tournament, Canadian pros, Ali, Joe Louis or a closed circuit bout between Sugar Ray Leonard and Roberto Duran.

When the Gardens was being built, boxing was envisioned as the major sports revenue stream after hockey and that was true until wrestling took hold. The Gardens "Friday Night Fights" were a popular attraction up to the mid-1950s.

The first amateur bouts, which included warmups for the 1932 Olympics in Los Angeles, were under way seven months after the building opened. The first pro fight on May 19, 1932, saw (Panama) Al Brown kayo Frenchman Emile (Spider) Pladner in less than two minutes. Joe Louis went four rounds with four different opponents in a 1935 exhibition.

Welterweight Sammy Luftspring, who would become well known in local boxing circles for years, was at his height as a fighter in this era, though Gordon Wallace won a split decision over him for the Canadian title in 1937. The year previous, in a protest anti-semitism in Germany, Luftspring was part of a boycott of a Gardens card of fighters going to Berlin.

Names in the 1930s, '40s and '50s who made several Gardens' appearances include Dave Castilloux, "Little" Arthur King and Alan McFater. King, a lightweight from Toronto, fought 18 times at the Gardens from 1946 to '48.

Chuvalo made his Gardens debut 10 years before the Ali fight, and cemented his reputation as a force in the heavyweight ranks by outslugging New Brunswick's Yvon Durelle on November 17, 1959 and moving right into a closed circuit match against Floyd Patterson. He also lost a close decision to WBA champ Terrell at the Gardens, before awaiting his shot at Ali.

 Gardens Gallery • Violent History

The site of the Gardens has a turbulent past that pre-dates Red Horner, Tiger Williams and Tie Domi. Richard Stromberg of Heritage Toronto says it's very likely the Gardens is located at the spot where shots were fired during the Rebellion of 1837. About 500 to 700 of William Lyon Mackenzie's insurgents were marching south down the winding road that was Yonge St. when they were met by gunfire from loyalists under Sherriff Jarvis on the Gardens side of the road. Both sides fled, but two men eventually were hanged for their role in the uprising.

WINSTON CHURCHILL

Eight years before the Battle Of Britain, Winston Churchill fought the Gardens' feeble sound system.

Not surprisingly, the great orator won, part of a triumphant visit here on March 3, 1932. Churchill addressed an audience of 6,000, an hour-long lecture.

A band played Rule Britannia as he entered and Churchill began speaking with the aid of a small lapel microphone. Foster Hewitt had warned the soldier-statesman that he needed a standard microphone to overcome the 11-second echo caused by the huge Gardens roof. Churchill, who had emptied director J.P. Bickell's wine cellar the night before, was in no mood to listen.

"Young man, when I want your advice, I'll ask for it," Churchill grumbled.

He also knocked over the floor mike Hewitt placed at his disposal after Churchill was introduced by former prime minister Arthur Meighen.

With his speech garbled by the echo and a weak loudspeaker, the audience began shouting 'turn it off, turn it off'.

"Can you hear me?" Churchill finally asked

"No," came a loud reply.

After trying to fix the mike, Churchill dispensed with it.

"I take no responsibility for the technical arrangements," he said. "But the resources of civilization being exhausted, I shall do the best I can on my own."

The *Telegram* reported "he was heard extraordinarily well after that in all parts of the arena."

Churchill spoke of the need for unity and strength in both the Empire and the United States and warned of trouble in Germany if its massive reparations bill from World War I was not eased. He also advocated the West not trade with the Russian "menace".

Gardens Events—1951

JAN. 29- FEB. 2, Ice Follies; FEB. 8, wrestling; FEB. 12, boxing; MARCH 18, Crippled Children's benefit; MARCH 21, first test TV broadcast of Leafs game; April 21, Bill Barilko's overtime goal wins the Leafs' seventh Cup; APRIL 23, boxing; JUNE 30, Ukrainian Jubilee; OCT. 1-6, Shrine circus; OCT. 9, NHL First all-star team vs. second team; OCT. 13, Afternoon exhibition game is played for the benefit of Princess Elizabeth.Chicago later beats the Leafs 3-1 in season opener; OCT. 23, first visit of Harlem Globetrotters; OCT. 29, Roy Ward Dixon; NOV. 12-16, Ice Capades.

Gardens Events—1952

JAN. 28 - FEB. 1, Ice Follies; FEB. 6, Leafs game cancelled due to death of King George VI; FEB. 15, Memorial service for the King; MARCH 3, Roy Ward Dixon; APRIL 6, Crippled Children's benefit; APRIL 22, Memorial Cup playoffs, Guelph beats Regina; APRIL 23-29, ice show with Barbara Ann Scott; MAY 6-8, Shrine convention; MAY 11, Canadian Peace Congress; MAY 26-29, Metropolitan Opera; JUNE 6, Cisco Kid's Western Roundup; AUG. 7, amateur wrestling; Sept. 20, Big Show of 1952; SEPT. 29 - OCT. 4, Shrine circus; OCT. 5, Mann Cup playoffs, Vancouver beats Peterborough; OCT. 11 1952-53 home opener, Chicago 6, Leafs 2; OCT. 14, boxing; OCT. 27, Roy Ward Dixon; OCT. 28, Dean Martin/Jerry Lewis; NOV. 10-14, Ice Capades.

42

GREAT MARLIES TEAMS

While the Leafs were monopolizing the Stanley Cup in the early 1960s, the Marlies built a powerhouse of their own at the Gardens. The 1963-64 club under Jim Gregory boasted a record of 40-9-7 en route to beating the Edmonton Oil Kings for the Memorial Cup.

Right winger Ron Ellis, centre Pete Stemkowski and left winger Wayne Carleton led the way with 130 goals and 121 assists in 56 games. That team sent a host of other players to the NHL, including Mike Walton, Rod Seiling and Jim McKenny.

Bobby Baun, a defenceman with the 1955 and '56 champions, said the Memorial Cup was more important to win than the Stanley Cup.

"You only have so many years (in junior), and to win two in a row is quite an accomplishment," Baun told the Sun's Tim Wharnsby. "If that team could've stayed together, we probably would have won four."

Baun's team, which faced down the Regina Pats both years for the title, was coached by Turk Broda and also featured Pulford, Bill Harris, Al MacNeil, Mike Nykoluk and Harry Neale.

Fast forward to 1971-72 when Dave Gardner, Bill Harris and Steve

Shutt became the first OHA Jr. A line to each record 50-goal seasons. Shutt had 70 in all.

The next year, the team also thrived on Bruce Boudreau, Paulin Bordeleau, Mark and Marty Howe, big Bob Dailey and goalie Mike Palmateer to win the Cup.

George Armstrong guided the team to its last title in 1975, a club that generated 469 goals, 105 points, but still faced elimination on seven occasions before winning the title. Mark Napier, a star on that team, now coaches the new St. Mike's junior entry which plays out of the Gardens.

Mark of Excellence: Mark Napier of the Marlies gets a unique shot on goal against Kitchener's Gord Laxton in Duke's 7-3 win to clinch their last Memorial Cup in 1975. (Barry Gray/The Toronto Sun)

43

KENNY DORATY ENDS LONG PLAYOFF GAME

The National Hockey League Guide and Record Book lists Ken Doraty's 1-0 overtime goal in Game 5 of the 1933 semi-finals against Boston as occurring April 3. In fact the goal came at 2 a.m. April 4, in the most drawn-out playoff game ever seen at the Gardens.

Six overtime periods finally came to an end at the 104-minute 46-second mark when Andy Blair picked off Eddie Shore's pass and set up Doraty in front of Bruins' goaltender Tiny Thompson.

The marathon was almost halted twice. After five overtimes, Smythe and Boston general manager Art Ross appealed to league president Frank Calder to continue the game the next day. But with the Rangers waiting to begin the Cup final the next evening, Calder said no.

Ross suggested a coin toss, which the Leafs ac-

cepted, but as the announcement was being made, a chorus of boos around the Gardens convinced both sides to continue. Calder tried to speed up matters by having both sides remove their goaltenders, but neither team was in favor.

It was left to Doraty, described as one of the lightest players in league history at 128 pounds, who'd been called up earlier that season to replace the injured Ace Bailey.

"He stood there for what seemed almost a minute," Foster Hewitt would recall of the decisive shot. By the time Doraty sent everyone home, a hoarse, mumbling Hewitt had passed out once and had lost eight pounds.

Doraty's record stood only three years, until Mud Bruneteau's goal at 116:30 of the sixth overtime led Detroit over the Montreal Maroons in a semi-final game.

KEN DORATY

GILMOUR'S SIX-ASSIST GAME

Doug Gilmour greatly simplified the task of passing Darryl Sittler's single season assist record on the eve of St. Valentine's Day, 1993.

He was in on all six goals the Leafs pumped by the Minnesota North Stars, tying a 49-year-old team record held by defenceman Babe Pratt and coming within one of a league record held jointly by Billy Taylor and Wayne Gretzky.

The six weren't cheap nor a gift from the official scorer. Five were first assists, the only second assist came as he was hit getting the puck out of the Leafs zone.

Gilmour said his first inclination of a record wasn't until the notice was posted on the scoreboard after his final assist.

By then, 15,720 fans were chanting "Dougie, Dougie".

"It's something I'll take in stride," Gilmour said. "My stats show I'm not a goal scorer, but my job is to make the plays."

Gilmour had done precisely that in 1992-93, his first full season in Toronto.

He bagged 95 assists in all, shattering Sittler's mark of 72 and going on to 127 points, 10 more than Sittler's best season.

In 392 regular season games, Gilmour had 321 assists, or .81 a game, compared to franchise leader Borje Salming's per game average of .56, with 620 in 1,099 games.

(Warren Toda/ Toronto Sun)

Gardens Events—1953

JAN. 8, wrestling; JAN. 27, pro tennis; FEB. 2-6, Ice Follies; FEB. 13, Gene Autry; MARCH 2, Roy Ward Dixon; MARCH 29, Crippled Children's benefit; APRIL 12, oldtimers hockey tournament; APRIL 13, Horace Heidt; APRIL 15, tennis; MAY 25-30, Metropolitan Opera; AUG. 7, Liberal Party rally; AUG. 21-22, Federated Women's Institutes pageant; SEPT. 18, Guard Republican Band of Paris; SEPT. 26, Biggest Show of 1953; OCT. 10, 1953-54 home opener, Leafs 6, Chicago 2; OCT. 27-29, ballet; NOV. 16-20, Ice Capades.

Gardens Events—1954

JAN. 20, pro tennis; JAN. 25, Youth For Christ meeting; FEB. 1-5, Ice Follies; MARCH 1; Roy Ward Dixon; Crippled Children's benefit; APRIL 27-MAY 1, Hollywood Ice Revue; MAY 8, Liberace; MAY 9, Memorial Cup playoffs, St. Catharines beats Edmonton; MAY 24-29, Metropolitan Opera; JUNE 14, Spike Jones; JULY 22, wrestling; SEPT. 27 - OCT. 2, Shrine circus; OCT. 5, Mantovani; OCT. 9, 1954-55 home opener, Leafs 3, Chicago 3; OCT. 18-20, ballet; NOV. 22-26, IceCapades; DEC. 14-16, Old Vic Company presents A Midsummer Night's Dream.

45

HAROLD BALLARD IN STATE

Harold Ballard hated to see the Gardens empty. So somewhere, he must have been smiling when hundreds of people—players, politicians and just plain folk—filed past his shiny mahogany closed casket in the directors lounge, five days after his death at age 86.

"He's probably thinking `they should have some of the concession stands open,'" former building treasurer Donald Crump wryly noted.

The casket was draped with a large blue and white banner, beneath huge portraits of Ballard and his wife Dorothy, who died in 1969.

The room was adorned with photographs of Ballard, his life and times at the Gardens and the team's glory years of the 1960s.
Nearby was the huge Canadian flag that flew over Parliament Hill on Ballard's 80th birthday, a gift from the federal government. Outside, the building's flags were at half mast, where they'd been lowered within an hour of his passing.

A Hamilton Tiger-Cats football helmet, representing Ballard's other love in pro sports and the only team that brought him a championship as sole owner, was placed near the coffin and beside it, a single red rose.

An Earfull: Harold Ballard playfully plugs his ears when fans booed him prior to a 1980 old timers game against Montreal. (Toronto Sun)

Wendel Clark, the most popular Leaf of the time, said he used his moment alone in the lounge to whisper a quiet thanks to Ballard for the opportunity to be a Leaf.

After the mayor, a cast of glory-era Leafs and delegations from the NHL and various teams paid their respects, it was the public's turn.

Lifelong Leaf fan Liam Horan of Toronto brought his six-year-old son William. "He was a legend and today is a little bit of history," Horan said.

GRETZKY AT THE GARDENS

Don't be surprised if the Maple Leafs offer to move the Gretzky family from Brantford to Vancouver or St. John's.

It has got something to do with No. 1 son Wayne trashing the Gardens every time he comes to town.

Of Gretzky's 160 points in 45 games against Toronto prior to 1998-99, the majority have come at the Gardens. Who can forget his virtuoso performance in Game 7 of the 1993 Western Conference final, the four-point night that busted the Leafs' Stanley Cup aspirations and foiled what would have been a Toronto Montreal Cup final?

"I love playing there," Gretzky said with a shrug when asked about his carnage on Carlton St. "It's a great building with so much tradition."

"But really, the biggest factor is that I'm playing in front of my family. I always want to be at my best when my Mom and Dad are watching."

Walter Gretzky was there when Wayne scored his first goal as a Brantford bantam. Then came jun-

ior success against the Toronto Marlboros as a Sault Ste. Marie Greyhound. But when Wayne merely glimpses Walter, Wayne's mother Phyllis or his three brothers and sister, it was usually bad news for the Leafs.

"It stands to reason that he won't disappoint his family and friends," Walter said.

Wayne had 10 points in his first two games at the Gardens and an incredible 20 goals and 20 assists in the 11 games by the 1985-86 season. At one stage, he was averaging 1.48 goals a game at the Gardens, compared to .86 as a visitor around the rest of the league.

"Wayne has a great feel for the history of the game," long-time Oiler public relations director Bill Tuele said. "So he likes to play in the arenas of the Original Six teams. He likes the atmosphere, the fact his family's there and he's always looking at the old pictures on the walls."

The irony for the Leafs of course is that Gretzky grew up primarily a Red Wings' fan.

Gardens Events—1955

JAN. 31 - FEB. 4, Ice Follies; APRIL 3, Timmy's Easter Parade of Stars; MAY 11, George Formby; MAY 23-28, Metropolitan Opera; AUG. 16-21; Churches of Christ convention; SEPT. 19, Mantovani; SEPT. 26-OCT. 1, Shrine circus; OCT. 2; Billy Graham Youth for Christ rally; OCT. 8, 1955-56 home opener, Leafs 4, Detroit 2; OCT. 11, Scots Guard band; OCT. 27, wrestling; NOV. 21-25, Ice Capades; DEC. 13-15, ballet.

Gardens Events—1956

JAN. 30 - FEB. 3, Ice Follies; MARCH 25, Timmy's Easter Parade of Stars; APRIL 23; Jack Dempsey's heavyweight tournament; APRIL 27, Memorial Cup final, Marlboros def. Regina; APRIL 30, First rockconcert, Bill Haley and his Comets; MAY 28-JUNE 2, Metropolitan Opera; JUNE 11, boxing; JULY 16, Rock and Roll Show; SEPT. 16, Mann Cup final, Nanaimo def. Peterborough; SEPT. 23, Diocese of Toronto meeting; SEPT. 29, Rock and Roll Show; OCT. 1-6, Shrine Circus; OCT. 13, 1956-57 home opener, Detroit 4, Leafs 1; OCT. 15-16, Royal Danish Ballet; OCT. 22, Boxing; NOV. 26-30, Ice Capades; DEC. 12, Billy Graham Crusade.

IAN TURNBULL'S FIVE-GOAL GAME

Ian Turnbull had great hands, whether it was passing and shooting or unwinding after games by playing guitar.

On this night, he made beautiful music at the Gardens to break a 59-year-old NHL scoring record by a defenceman in one game.

It was five shots, five goals on Detroit netminders Ed Giacomin and Jim Rutherford in a 9-1 win, a feat unsurpassed by a rearguard heading into the 1998-99 season.

"It was like a good day at the track," said Turnbull, who once scored five in a game for the Montreal Jr. Canadiens.

Like Darryl Sittler's 10-point night almost a year to the day, Turnbull had been in a slump, and broke out in a huge way.

Ironically, the first period was scoreless until Turnbull banked a shot off Terry Harper past Giacomin at 1:55 of the second. No. 2 was on a

breakaway after Turnbull intercepted a pass. Defensive partner Borje Salming helped complete the third-period hat trick with a perfect pass up the middle.

Salming, knowing some kind of record was in reach, had told Turnbull after the fourth goal to keep hanging around centre and wait for a pass. Salming also urged him to go for a sixth goal, but time ran out.

But Salming broke his own single season Leafs record for points by a defenceman that night, noteworthy because Turnbull spent much of his Leafs career in Salming's shadow.

Turnbull, though a headstrong player and a challenge to his coaches, would prove his worth in the 1978 playoffs when Salming went out with an eye injury.

When he was traded in 1981 to Los Angeles, his 414 points were third among club defencemen, behind only Salming and Tim Horton.

Tea for Turnbull: Ian Turnbull and his wife, Inge, accept a silver tea service to mark his record five-goal game by a defenceman. (Barry Gray/Toronto Sun)

48

CONCERTS, '70S, THE CPI YEARS

To get into the building in the 1970s, you either had to meet Harold Ballard's price for a Leafs' ticket or go through his enterprising son Bill to watch a concert.

A vice-president of the Gardens before he turned 30, Bill's hustle as attractions manager steered a number of premier concerts to the building. In 1974, he resigned, joined partners in buying out his father's share of the entertainment arm of the Gardens and formed Concert Productions International.

A new deal with the Gardens was struck, with roughly 25% of the gross going to rent. CPI virtually cornered the year-round big-ticket live concert scene in Toronto until the SkyDome was built in 1989.

Concert notables —Led Zeppelin (9/4/71);Yes (10/31/72)...Neil Young (1/15/73); Frank Zappa (5/4/73); Bob Dylan and The Band (1/10/74); Elton John (11/18/74); George Harrison (12/6/74); Genesis (12/16/74);Alice Cooper (5/2/75); Rolling Stones (6/17-18/75);Who (12/11/75); Supertramp (4/20/76); Paul McCartney and Wings (5/9/76); Queen (2/1/77); Eagles (3/30/77)...Chicago (10/31/77); Eric Clapton (4/9/78); David Bowie (5/1/78); Neil Diamond (7/30-31/78); Bruce Springsteen (11/16/78); Rush (12/28-30/78); Rod Stewart (5/6-7/79); Steve Martin (7/29/79); Bob Marley (11/1/79).

Don Felder of The Eagles (top, Mike Peake/ Toronto Sun) and Bob Marley (Jonathon Gross/Toronto Sun) entertain fans at the Gardens in the '70s.

RELIGIOUS MEETINGS

Often described as a hockey temple, the Gardens was used for an incredible number of religious meetings of all denominations.

So many people came to see the Rev. Billy Graham's four-day crusade at the Gardens in 1978 that Graham came outside to address some of the estimated 8,000 who couldn't fit in. Two years later, the Baptist World Congress drew 20,000.

When the Rev. Jimmy Swaggart came to the Gardens, he completely enthralled Harold Ballard, not only with the strength of his convictions, but his ability to get people to open their wallets.

But Ballard wasn't about to get outhustled in his own backyard and sent an emmisary to collect a royalty on Swaggart's bible sales within the Gardens.

Prior to World War II, the Gardens had been

packed to hear spell-binding evangelist Aimee Semple McPherson, the Salvation Army Congress as well as being host to the Canadian Jewish Congress in 1938, with the intolerance of Nazism the main topic.

A hockey temple: An Anglican rally in 1956. (The Toronto Telegram)

Gardens Events—1957

JAN. 28 - FEB. 1, Ice Follies; FEB. 18, Rock and Roll Show; MARCH 16, Leafs record 14 goals vs. Rangers; MARCH 25, boxing; APRIL 2, Elvis Presley; APRIL 14, Perry Como; APRIL 23, Allan Cup, Whitby vs. Spokane; APRIL 29, Rock And Roll Show; MAY 25, Pat Boone; MAY 27-JUNE 1, Metropolitan Opera; JUNE 4, Liberal party rally; SEPT. 14, Rock and Roll Show; SEPT. 26, Scottish pipe bands; SEPT. 30 - OCT. 5, Shrine circus; OCT. 12, 1957-58 home opener, Detroit 5, Leafs 3; NOV. 22, International hockey, Whitby 7, Russia 2; NOV. 25-30, Ice Capades.

Gardens Events—1958

JAN. 13 -15, ballet; JAN. 20, Rock and Roll Show; FEB. 3-7, Ice Follies; MARCH 30, Timmy's Easter Parade Of Stars; APRIL 21, Rock and Roll Show; MAY 6, Pro tennis; MAY 9-10, Moiseyev ballet; MAY 26-31, Metropolitan Opera; JUNE 29, Baptist Youth World Concert; SEPT. 15, boxing; SEPT. 24, Scottish pipe bands; SEPT. 29-OCT. 4, Shrine circus; OCT. 11, 1958-59 home opener, Chicago 3, Leafs 1; OCT. 21, Maria Callas; NOV. 3-7; Ice Capades; DEC. 29, Toronto amateur indoor soccer.

POLITICAL RALLIES

To create the biggest, noisiest show possible, political parties of all stripes chose the most famous arena in the country for rallies and leadership conventions.

Six prime ministers had starring roles at the Gardens, though Pierre Trudeau suffered a near-defeat in the 1972 election after a rock-oriented rally that saw the group Crowbar get more cheers than he did. He briefly lost his job in 1979 following another loud Liberal show for 18,000 that preceded a severe beating by Joe Clark.

The Tories dominated headlines in 1967 when they gathered for a leadership vote that unexpectedly toppled warhorse John Diefenbaker and replaced him with Robert Stanfield. But Stanfield's moment in the sun was brief, from the infamous banana picture at the Gardens, to three straight defeats at the hands of Trudeau in the ensuing seven years.

Prime Minister Louis St. Laurent was a Liberal leader who did do well by the Gardens through appearances in the 1940s and '50s. He returned one last time to open the 1961-62 season and his magic rubbed off on the Leafs, who won three consecutive Cups from that point.

Mackenzie King knew what the people liked in 1935 when he brought multi-sports star Lionel Conacher, brother of Leafs' Charlie, to speak briefly to a Liberal fest. King, the challenger to Prime Minister R. B. Bennett was riding a wave of popularity then and mounted police were needed to control gate crashers around the building.

Bennett got a predictably cooler response from a Depression-weary crowd when the Conservatives came in the next night. Just 48 hours later, the short-lived Reconstruction Party drew 10,000 people to the Gardens, though its leader Harry Stevens, and its grassroots platform never caught on.

Other notable Canadian politicians to speak at the Gardens included the once-banned Tim Buck, leader of the Communist party, whose visit saw RCMP officers combing the crowd taking pictures.

International lectures featured Winston Churchill and U.S. presidential candidate Wendell Wilkie. Senator Robert Kennedy, a good friend of the Bassett family, dropped by informally one night through the Hot Stove entrance and was almost barred by a waiter who didn't recognize him.

Loud Crowd: The Gardens was the site of many raucous political meetings, rallies and conventions, such as this Liberal rally in 1957.

51

GREAT CAPTAINS

Sixteen Maple Leafs, eight of them now residing in the Hall Of Fame, benefited from a healthy shot of Vitamin C.

From Day to Keon to Clark to Gilmour there was something about being captain of the Leafs that made you play taller.

"You are not named captain of a team unless you have some leadership qualities," Darryl Sittler said at Clark's swearing-in ceremony. "But I didn't change just because I was named captain. The thing you have to do is include other players with leadership qualities.

Wendel (Clark) did that with Doug, I did it with Lanny McDonald and Tiger Williams."

Charlie (The Big Bomber) Conacher and George (The Chief) Armstrong, two captains

whose combined careers covered five decades, had their sweater numbers honored the same evening at the Gardens, February 28, 1998.

In putting Conacher's No. 9 and Armstrong's No. 10 in the rafters, the Leafs also recognized two Hall of Famers and two of the finest right wingers the game has seen. Conacher scored the first Leafs' goal in Gardens history,

Armstrong played the most games, 1,187, and scored the last goal in Toronto's 1967 Cup victory.

"I must have been a better player than I thought I was," Armstrong said in typical aw-shucks fashion to the *Sun*'s Dave Fuller. But tears welled up in the four-time Cup winner's eyes as his banner was raised.

Armstrong won two Memorial Cups in the 1970s with the Toronto Marlboros and served as coach of the Leafs in 1988-89. He still works for the Leafs as a scout.

In Conacher's 459 regular season games, he compiled an impressive 398 points.

A member of the great Kid Line, he's the only Leaf to win the NHL scoring title back-to-back (1933-34 and '34-35) and he and Babe Dye are the only Leafs to win it more than once.

The 205-pound Conacher had a wicked wrist shot that sometimes got out of control. Padding wasn't very thick in those days and there were fears he'd killed Ranger goalie John Ross Roach in the '32 playoffs with one such drive in the chest. Other victims included his brother Lionel, then a Montreal Maroons defenceman.

"C" of happiness: New Leafs captain Darryl Sittler is flanked by predecessors George Armstrong and Bob Davisson. (Barry Gary/The Toronto Sun)

52

WRESTLING IN THE '60s AND '70s

The Tunneys often were asked the secret of their Gardens success, but it may have been nothing more than creative carpentry.

"They always said you should have a ramp leading to the ring, so that the fighters would always be above the crowd," Zarlenga said. "It wasn't hard to build one, and the visual effect was so great."

The ethnicity of the wrestlers also was promoted in multicultural Toronto. Thus, fighters such as Spiros Arion carried the Greek banner, Bruno Sammartino and Dominic DeNucci were heroes to the sizable Italian community, while Tiger Jeet Singh and Mickey Doyle were adopted by the Indian and Irish fans respectively.

"When Italy won the World Cup of soccer, a little-known wrestler was sent out before the card waving a big Italian flag," Zarlenga recalled with a smile.

"The crowd went absolutely nuts. I forget the wrestler's name, but if he didn't win up to then, I bet he won that night."

The Sheik, with his equally despised manager Abdulah (The Weasel) Farouk, was a fixture in the Gardens in the 70s. A series of challengers; Tiger Jeet Singh, Tex McKenzie, Bobo Brazil, Haystack Calhoun, Terry Funk and venerable Lord Athol Layton, all attempted to outwit his camel clutch.

Three wrestling organzations, the NWA, WWF and AWA, were on the scene by the late '70s, with Harley Race, Nick Bockwinkle, Superstar Bly Graham, Pat Patterson and Angelo Mosca sharing the centre stage.

In 1978 Frank Tunney signed an exclusivity agreement with the NWA, which quickly locked up all the recognized stars. That culminated in a bout between Ric (Nature Boy) Flair and Ricky Steamboat in the autumn of '78, a 48-minute curfew draw generally regarded as the best match ever held at the Gardens.

Gardens Gallery • Fill 'er up

In the course of a season, which usually includes 41 home games, about 10 exhibition and playoff matches and two or three practices a week, the Leafs training staff goes through an incredible amount of Gardens' supplies. A typical year will see a player use 150 sticks, two or three pairs of skates, get 125 skate sharpenings, and five pairs of gloves. The team downs 2,000 litres of Gatorade, uses 7,500 rolls of tape, 2,000 bars of soap and 30,000 sticks of gum.

53

CONCERTS OF THE '80s AND '90s

Musical tastes changed as the soppy '70s gave way to punk, new wave, eventually followed by grunge, rap, new country and other alternative styles.

But the new blood also was drawn to the Gardens, which still attracted the famous names from the previous 20 years.

The Gardens entered the '90s in competition with new venues for an increasingly shrinking tour market. By 1998, business was drying up.

Concert notables: Bruce Springsteen (1/20-21/81); Elvis Costello (2/9/81); AC/DC (12/10-11/81); The Who (12/16-17/82); Neil Young (2/18/83); The Clash (4/30/84); U2 (3/28/85); Madonna (5/23/85); Paul Simon (6/23-24/87); Bryan Adams (6/29/87); Prince (10/5/88); Neil Diamond (2/9-10/89); Garth Brooks (10/4/91); U2 (3/24/92); Eric Clapton (10/5-6/94); Pearl Jam (9/21/96); Tragically Hip (12/12-13/96); Lord Of The Dance (5/4-5/97); Oasis (1/15/98).

Queen (top) and Elton John were among the performers to entertain at the Gardens in the '80s. (Toronto Sun)

54

SPRINGSTEEN

ormer *Toronto Sun* music critic Wilder Penfield III and *Sun* entertainment editor Bob Thompson covered two decades of the Gardens' concert business at its peak. Asked to compile a list of the best entertainers they'd seen at the Gardens, both put Bruce Springsteen at the top, though Thompson called Neil Young's 1986 appearance the best full concert he'd seen, with The Boss's 45-minute set during the Amnesty International benefit in 1988 a close second.

Penfield wrote of Springsteen's 1977 Gardens show: "The hardest act to follow in music is his own first act." Twenty years later, Penfield hadn't changed his mind.

"One year in Toronto, he played 2½ hours of songs everyone knew the words to, took a break and played an hour of oldies. He's the greatest live performer I've ever seen."

Though Young made several Gardens stops, beginning in January 1973 when he became the first homegrown singer to sell out the building, Thompson says October 3, 1986 was a highwater mark.

"That tour did a lot of surprising material," Thompson said. "That night it was Mr. Soul, a Buffalo Springfield song he never did and Cinnamon Girl, which he'd played occasionally. I wrote that night that he gave rock'n'roll a reason to have a history."

Penfield's second choice was The Who.

"There was just so much tension on stage, but it exploded into great music," Penfield said of their concerts here, which included a much hyped, but ultimately premature final appearance. "Pick any show when (drummer) Keith Moon was still alive."

Boss of Gardens: Bruce Springsteen

55

BEST OF THE REST CONCERTS

Penfield and Thompson compiled other high lights from their years at the Gardens.

- U2 - "Their Gardens show (in 1985) was their first arena tour and everyone was waiting to see if they could pull it off"Thompson said.
- Bob Marley - "A real incantatory power," Penfield said. You could feel the whole building pulsating to 'Get Up, Stand Up'. It's the closest the Gardens has ever come to feeling like a small club."
- Queen - "Always a great light show, Penfield said. "One year it was robot controlled and it kept swooping in on them."
- John Cougar Mellencamp - "The 1987 show was the first kind of overwhelming respect he received,"Thompson said. "There were fiddles, acoustic guitars; a lot of rootsy creativity."
- Rolling Stones: "They were on a stage that looked like a mother of pearl," Penfield said. "They had a 40-foot inflated phallic symbol (which had broken loose and floored special guest keyboard player Billy Preston at a previous concert). All of them were at their best."
- AC/DC: "The last time they were here, I couldn't believe the power of Angus Young's guitar,"Thompson said. "It was so crisp. He was playing rock."
- Prince: "He had a speaker at the back set up so he could talk to himself playing the role of God," Penfield said.

Honorable mention— Peter Gabriel, R.E.M., Bee Gees, the annual Rush shows on New Year's Eve, Paul McCartney, Madonna, Led Zeppelin, Jimmy Buffett, Jackson Five, Chicago, and Pink Floyd.

Prince of Gardens: Prince performs in 1984. (Hug Wesley/ Toronto Sun)

56

RICK VAIVE'S 50 GOALS

Once he got into the 50-goal habit, Rick Vaive found it a hard one to break.

After the franchise waited 65 years for its first 50-goal sniper, Vaive did it three years in a row, starting this night at the Gardens against the St. Louis Blues. Vaive's 54 goals in 1981-82 also became the team record.

Vaive was acquired from Vancouver in 1980, an unpopular trade at the time that saw fan favorites Tiger Williams and Jerry Butler leave. Vaive arrived with centre Bill Derlago, a crafty centre, who would figure very large in Vaive's 299 career goals as a Leaf.

A native of Prince Edward Island, the right winger preferred using a heavy stick.

"It looked like a log" teammate Gary Leeman would joke. But goaltenders found nothing funny about the booming shot Vaive could unleash.

Several Leafs had flirted with 50, most notably Frank Mahovlich with 48 in the 1960-61 season. It wasn't until the mid-seventies that other Leafs would come close, Errol Thompson's 43, followed by Lanny McDonald's 46 and 47.

Then came Vaive's big year, in which he'd account for 18% of the team's goals, in his first year as team captain. As a warmup two nights before,

Vaive had a hat trick at the Gardens against the Blackhawks to reach 49 and pass Mahovlich.

At 14:57 of the first period, Derlago weaved through two Blues and fed an uncovered Vaive on his wrong wing during a power play. Vaive snapped the puck home before goaltender Mike Liut could move.

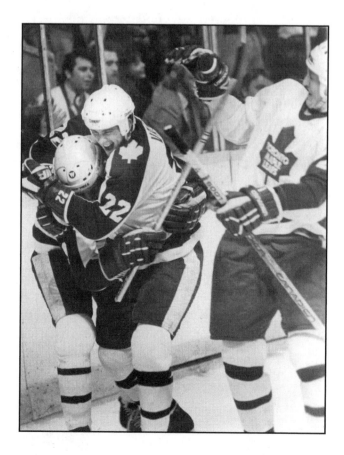

Record Re-vaive-al: Rick Vaive celebrates his 50th goal of the 1981-82 season, a first for the Leafs. (Barry Gray/The Toronto Sun)

57

GREAT LEAFS COACHES

The two-foot-high platform behind the Leafs bench can make a coach feel like he's on top of the world. Or walking the plank.

Few of the 25 men who've paced it departed on their own terms, yet most consider even the shortest of stays to be an honor.

Nine Hall Of Famers have coached the Leafs, led by Punch Imlach with his 365 wins and a like number of superstitions. It wasn't uncommon to see him walking down the hallways in the same suit he'd worn for days as good luck, touching every doorknob and emptying his wallet of the unlucky $2 bills.

Art Duncan was the coach the night the building opened, but was replaced just six games later by Dick Irvin, who won the Cup. Roger Neilson was fired and rehired in 48 hours and nearly was forced to wear a bag over his head in his return.

King Clancy went behind the bench on three occasions over three decades, Pat Burns consistently was voted the best-dressed coach in the league as well as winning the Jack Adams Trophy twice. Future Hall of Famer Pat Quinn will take the Leafs into 2000.

But the most colorful had to be John Brophy, with language as blue as the Leafs sweater. The man who liked to screen movies such as Patton and sleep in his office set an unofficial record with a post-game harangue that included 72 cuss words in four minutes.

Brophy's boys: John Brophy was among the most colorful of Leafs coaches. (Bill Sandford/The Toronto Sun)

58

MARLIES/PETERBOROUGH GAME

A **crowd** of 16,485 watched the deciding game of the Ontario Major Junior Hockey League series, still a record attendance for a junior match .

One of the most powerful Toronto teams of all time came into this game with a 10-4-2 playoff record, needing just a tie to wrap up the eight-point series.

The Marlies did it in dramatic fashion, rallying from a 5-4 deficit on a penalty shot goal by Paulin Bordeleau after Petes' defenceman Jim Turkiewicz handled the puck in the crease.

"You talk to anyone from Peterborough today and they'll still tell you (Turkiewicz) never touched the puck," Bonello said with a laugh. "We had such a huge rivalry with Peterborough."

Gardens Events—1959

FEB. 2-6, Ice Follies; MARCH 22, Timmy's Easter Parade Of Stars; APRIL 19, Allan Cup finals, Vernon versus Whitby; APRIL 20, Pro tennis; APRIL 28, Benny Goodman Orchestra; MAY 25-30, Metropolitan Opera; JUNE 11-13, Bolshoi Ballet; AUG. 25-27, Russian Festival of Music; SEPT. 21, Tom Jones, Engelbert Humperdinck; SEPT. 28 - OCT. 3, Shrine circus; OCT. 10, 1959-60 home opener, Leafs 6, Chicago 3; NOV. 9-13, Ice Capades; NOV. 17, Boxing; NOV. 22, Boxing (first use of closed circuit TV); NOV. 26-27, Polish ballet.

Gardens Events—1960

JAN. 19, International hockey, Moscow vs. Whitby; FEB. 2-5, Ice Follies; FEB. 9, Moscow State Symphony; FEB. 15, Pro tennis; FEB. 22, Toronto Symphony; FEB. 23, Fred Waring and his Pennsylvanians; MARCH 4, International hockey, Czechoslovkia vs. Whitby; MARCH 16-18, Timmy's Easter Parade Of Stars; APRIL 29, Memorial Cup playoffs, St. Catharines versus Edmonton; MAY 13-14, Georgia Dance Co.; MAY 30, Metropolitan Opera; SEPT. 26-OCT. 4, Lions Club circus; OCT. 8' 1960-61 home opener, Rangers 5, Leafs 2; OCT. 12, Count Basie and Stan Kenton; OCT. 31, Rock and Roll Show; NOV. 7-11, Ice Capades.

Gardens Gallery • Bowled Over

One of the most intriguing stops on a tour of the Gardens is the six-lane bowling alley that runs almost the length of the East greens under the seats.

Part of the original construction plans, it was thought the sport was ready to take off. Some tournaments were run, but like the billiards room that was also in the plans and the gymnasium, it was converted to storage space.

59

ACE BAILEY TRIBUTE GAME

February 14, 1934

When Eddie Shore extended his hand to Irvine (Ace) Bailey at centre ice prior to this game, about 14,000 people held their breath.

But the Gardens broke into applause when Bailey shook the hand and exchanged a few words to show he'd forgiven the man who had violently ended his career and nearly killed him two months earlier.

Bailey was a fine right winger with 193 points in 313 games when the Leafs made a fateful trip to Boston on the night of December 12.

Shore, one of the meanest men in the game on or off the ice, had been tripped by King Clancy and become enraged when no penalty was called. Either mistaking Bailey for Clancy or determined to hurt the first Leaf he saw, Shore rammed the Leaf from behind, sending him tumbling through the air. Bailey's bare head bounced off the ice with a terrible splat.

Bailey's legs began to twitch and the doctor at the game quickly ascertained he'd suffered a seri-

Truce: Eddie Shore and Ace Bailey (left) shake hands prior to the Bailey Benefit that would later become the All-Star Game. (Hockey Hall of Fame)

ous head injury. Shore wasn't feeling very good himself, after Leaf Red Horner slugged him in the jaw when the Bruin showed no remorse. Shore split his head open as he fell to the ice, leaving medical attendants with two unconscious players to deal with.

At the hospital, Bailey was fortunate to have a top neurosurgeon on duty.

Two operations a week apart were needed to clear a blood clot, though Bailey almost died from swallowing his tongue.

Thousands of get-well messages arrived at the Boston hospital, where the recovering Bailey was considering assault charges against Shore and suing him. But the doctor who saved his life advised Bailey against that, warning he'd see $5000 at the most. The doctor had heard of a special night back at the Gardens being planned on Bailey's behalf and urged him to temper his anger.

With the Leafs lined up against a collection of top NHLers, including Shore, the two men made peace prior to the game.

National Hockey League All-Stars vs. the Toronto Maple Leafs in the Ace Bailey Benefit Game, February 14, 1934. (Hockey Hall of Fame)

"I was never the type of man to hold grudges against anybody," Bailey told author Brian McFarlane.

Toronto beat the NHLers 7-3 and raised $20,909.40 for Bailey, added to $7,800 in gate re-ceipts from a Bruins-Maroons tribute match.

The game's format became the model for a regular "all-star game", that would pit the previous year's Stanley Cup champions against the league's best players.

Gardens Events–1961

JAN. 30, Ice Follies; FEB. 11, Tim Horton's streak of 468 consecutive games begins; MARCH 13, closed circuit boxing; MARCH 26, Timmy's Easter Parade of Stars; APRIL 29, Pro tennis; MAY 26-27, Moiseyev Dance Co.; MAY 30 - JUNE 3, Ringling Bros., Barnum and Bailey Circis; JUNE 22, wrestling; JUNE 27, boxing; JULY 2-6 Kiwanis International Convention; AUG. 25-31, Red Army singers and dancers; SEPT. 2, Latvian song festival; OCT. 8, Dick Clark's Caravan of Stars; OCT. 14, 1960-61 home opener, Leafs 3, Boston 2; OCT. 22-25, Leningrad ballet; NOV. 6-10, Ice Capades; DEC. 4, boxing; DEC. 12-13, Polish song and dance company.

Gardens Events—1962

JAN. 29 - FEB. 2, Ice Follies; FEB. 19, Chubby Checker; MARCH 21, Evening with Gershwin; APRIL 15, Timmy's Easter Parade of Stars; APRIL 25 - 28, Rotary Ice Revue; MAY 25-26, Ukrainian Dance Company; MAY 27, Rotary musical concert; MAY 29 - JUNE 3, Ringling Bros., Barnum and Bailey Circus; SEPT. 4-16, Moscow Circus; SEPT. 25, Floyd Patterson Vs. Sonny Liston (CC); OCT. 6, Maple Leafs beat NHLall-stars 4-1; OCT. 13, home opener, Leafs and Bruins tie, 2-2; NOV. 5-11, Ice Capades; NOV. 20, Scottish pipe bands; NOV. 23, touring Russian national hockey team exhibition; DEC. 10-13, Bolshoi ballet.

Gardens Gallery • Pyramid Power

In the 1976 playoffs against the Philadelphia Flyers, the Leafs bench and dressing room looked like a Cairo gift shop.

Coach Red Kelly, intrigued by stories that pyramids contained ancient and mystical forces, stuck them high and low around the Gardens, in the room and under the bench.

When captain Darryl Sittler put his sticks beneath one in the room and scored five goals, the whole city went pyramid crazy.

It may all have been a motivational ploy by Kelly to counteract the Flyers' powerful charm, singer Kate (God Bless America) Smith. Kelly's story wound up on many science-fiction programs, but the Leafs lost the series in seven games.

60

LOCAL COLOR

Televised baseball games the past 10 or 15 years gave audiences the impression that Toronto fans must be among the most reserved in the world.

But the Gardens has been home to plenty of memorable characters and leather lungs over the years, going back to opening night in 1931 when the premier and mayor were heckled during their speeches.

Those were the days when a few hundred standing room seats would go on sale for about a buck or less at game time, attracting a different, livelier type of fan than the many stuffed shirts at railside. There'd be a minor stampede up the stairs when the gates opened for standing room as people jockeyed for the best spots.

In the greys "it was like the bleachers at a ball game in Chicago," veteran usher Dennis Goodwin said. "You almost had a miniature Hot Stove League going on game nights, with little side bets between ushers or between ushers and fans, a quarter or a dollar on who'd get the first goal or penalty."

There were a few memorable voices closer to the ice, such as the guy in the west reds who faithfully shouted "C'Mon Teeder!" for the captain of the early 1950s. Norm Ullman had the same one-man fan club two decades later and another would give an exaggerated "Hail Caesar" each time ex-Leaf Cesare Maniago made an appearance.

Being a superstar didn't earn visitors such as Bobby Orr a break. No. 4 was booed loudly everytime he touched the puck, a razzing that Mario Lemieux and Eric Lindros also were accorded. Only Wayne Gretzky got a consistently warm reception.

Wrestling fans still look back with fondness on an elderly woman who sat above the performers' exit and whacked any grappler she didn't like with her umbrella.

 Gardens Gallery • Ouch!

When a vulcanized rubber puck, travelling more than than 100 miles per hour, leaves the playing surface and lands a split-second later in the first few rows of a sold-out building, someone is bound to get hurt. Before Gardens glass was raised a few inches in the 1990s, partly in response to puck-related injuries, two to six people on average were struck a game. The puck isn't choosey about its victims, either. A doctor on call at the Gardens once had to tend to his wife, who wound up needing $5,000 of dental surgery when struck in the mouth. Coach Pat Burns was dinged once, as was Leafs trainer Brent Smith, who is usually the first one to throw a towel into the stands to help a bleeding patron.

61

TORONTO TOROS

A **long**-time argument in Toronto was whether the city could support two professional hockey teams.

Between 1973 and '76, people got a pretty good idea, with the Gardens as the battleground. The World Hockey Association arrived on the scene, attracting a mixture of the young and the curious among hockey fans.

"It was like New York; we were the Mets and the Leafs were the Yankees," former Toros' boss Gilles Leger said with a chuckle.

Ballard wasted no time stirring the pot, charging the Toros a hefty $15,000 a game rent, then surprising them with an additional $3,500 bill on opening night to turn on the TV lights. Then he

Toros' Frank Mahovlich struggles to get into scoring position during a playoff game at the Gardens. (Barry Gray/The Toronto Sun)

drained them for about $100,000 to build a new dressing room in the bowels of the northwest corner, which is still used by visiting NHL teams.

"We had some good times," Leger maintained. "The WHA was really wide-open hockey and we had a lot of names familiar to fans here; Paul Henderson, Frank Mahovlich, Carl Brewer, Wayne Dillon and Gilles Gratton."

The Toros made a huge fuss when (Shot Gun) Tom Simpson scored 50 goals a year before any Leaf managed the feat. But the team had no more luck bringing a title here than the Leafs and eventually moved to Birmingham, Alabama.

Gardens Gallery • First Leafs Victory

Heading into the 1998-99 season, the Leafs had played 2,081 games at the Gardens, with a record of 1,196-760-344. Though their opening night 2-1 loss to Chicago is well documented, the first Leafs win on Gardens ice came Nov. 28, 1931 when Red Horner scored at 1:45 of overtime in a 4-3 win over Boston.

BIG MARGIN LEAF WINS

In the low scoring NHL of the late 1990s, it's possible that a team could play five or six games over two weeks and not get 14 goals.

But on March 16, 1957, at the Gardens, the Leafs swarmed Gump Worsley and the Rangers 14-1, the most goals the team ever has had in one game.

Led by hat tricks from Sid Smith and Brian Cullen, the Leafs racked up 23 assists and 37 scoring points. Todd Sloan and Ron Stewart had two each. Every Leaf, with the exception of defenceman Jim Thomson and goalie Broda ended up on the scoresheet.

Toronto took 47 shots on the beleaguered Worsley. Ironically the Leafs were up just 2-0 early in the second.

A 13-0 drubbing of Detroit on January 2, 1971, was the largest goose egg margin in Leafs history. Detroit was handed its worst defeat ever.

Norm Ullman and Paul Henderson burned the Wings with two goals and two assists, with Jim Harrison notching four assists, two on goals by a rookie named Darryl Sittler.

The Leafs had to change to Bruce Gamble in net when Jacques Plante bumped his head on the ice. On the Wings side, Howe and Frank Mahovlich were early scratches with injuries. Don McLeod eventually replaced starting goalie Jim Rutherford.

Gardens Events—1963

JAN. 24, wrestling; JAN. 25, Telegram/Maple Leaf indoor games; JAN. 28-FEB. 2, Ice Follies; FEB. 11, Trail Smoke Eaters vs. University all-stars; FEB. 25, Pro tennis; MARCH 29, NDP convention; APRIL 1, Timmy's Easter Parade Of Stars; APRIL 9, Dick Duff's record two playoff goals in first 68 seconds; APRIL 18, Leafs beat Detroit 3-1 to win ninth Stanley Cup; JUNE 1, Diocesan Eucharistic Day Mass; JULY 9, Tommy Dorsey Orchestra; JULY 19, Dick Clark Show; JULY 22, boxing, Patterson vs Liston (CC); AUG. 13, World Anglican Congress; AUG. 18, Anglican Congress; AUG. 31, Country music show; SEPT. 17, Black Watch Band; SEPT. 30-OCT. 6, Don Ameche's circus; OCT. 5, Leafs tie NHL all-stars 3-3; OCT. 12, 1963-64 season opener, Leafs 5, Boston 1; OCT. 18, Hootenanny; NOV. 5-12, Ice Capades; NOV. 21-22, Olympic figure skating trials; NOV. 24-29, Canadian championship rodeo; DEC. 29, Canada - Sweden exhibition hockey.

Gardens Gallery • Picture Perfect

The Leafs never had room for a team Hall of Fame at the Gardens, but created one by accident. Unlike the other Original Six buildings, whose walls were bare or cluttered with ads, the Leafs started a collection of vintage photographs that eventually wrapped the ground floor in a wonderful gallery of memories. The mostly black and white pictures, which include the Cup teams, action shots and individual portraits, never failed to draw a crowd. With more than 30 years between Cups, they were a thread joining the Leafs' dynasty. "Those pictures were one of the great things about visiting the Gardens, for a player or a fan," Red Kelly said. "You walk down the hall, look around and say, 'I played with him, or I remember that guy, or I listened to him on radio,' You knew you were in a hockey building."

63

THE GARDENS GOES TO WAR

Conn Smythe, a World War I gunner who rose to the rank of lieutenant, put his building and his employees on full alert during 1939-45. Twenty two Leafs served in World War II, including Syl Apps and Turk Broda.

Smythe organized his own battalion, the 30th Sportsmen's Battery, an amalgam of athletes, sports writers and Gardens workers, but while he was away the building was host of numerous events in connection with the war effort.

There were bond rallies, bingo nights, political speakers, military marches and war games, complete with hand-to-hand combat demos and machine guns mounted at centre ice. The Dionne quintuplets visited one such pageant in 1942 and American stars

Getting the point: The Gardens was used extensively as a military parade ground and training base in World War II. (City of Toronto Archives)

such as Bob Hope, the Andrews Sisters and Fibber McGee and Molly came to the Gardens for the Allied cause. Hope's show in 1944 was attended by several wounded veterans. A Milk For Britain fund-raiser was also organized.

Soldiers in uniform usually were charged less to attend Gardens events and many distinguished military personnel performed the opening face-off of each new NHL season.

Private Alex Chisholm, decorated for heroism at Dieppe, did the honors for the 1942-43 season. At war's end, six Victoria Cross winners; Cpl. Fred Topham, Pvt. Smoky Smith, Major Fred Tilson, Lt. Col. Paul Triquet, Lt. Col. D.V. Currie and Maj. J.J. Mahoney presided at the 1945-46 opener.

64

HOWIE MEEKER'S FIVE-GOAL ROOKIE GAME

f Howie Meeker didn't look too excited at setting an NHL record with five goals in one game, there was good reason.

Meeker skated off the ice following the 10-4 romp over Chicago thinking he'd scored only three.

His first two were credited to Wally Stanowski. In the first period the latter's shot hit Meeker in the shin and he blindly fired it behind Hawks goalie Paul Bibeault. Meeker didn't dispute the announcement that Stanowski had scored.

Another Stanowski shot in the second period banked in off Meeker's butt as Johnny Mariucci cross-checked him.

When Meeker came to the bench after scoring a few minutes later on passes from Teeder

Meeker makes five: Leafs coach Hap Day (left), had a hand in Howie Meeker's record five goals in one game by a rookie. (The Toronto Sun)

Kennedy and Joe Klukay, he told Klukay he thought he had the two earlier. Coach Hap Day overheard him and secretly notified the official scorer to review Stanowski's goals, while Meeker added two more in the third.

Meeker was stunned when his wife congratulated him on a five-goal game afterward, quickly seeking out Day to thank him. The only other NHL rookie to get five in one night through the 1997-98 season was the Rangers' Don Murdoch in 1976.

Meeker went on to score 27 goals in 55 games and win the Calder Trophy, beating out Gordie Howe. He coached the Leafs in 1956-57 and later embarked on a four-decade Hall of Fame career in broadcasting that lasted until 1998.

Gardens Events—1964

JAN. 1-4, curling; JAN. 5; Sweden - Czechoslovakia exhibition hockey; JAN. 24; Telegram/Maple Leaf indoor games; JAN. 27-FEB. 2, Ice Follies; FEB. 25, Liston vs. Cassius Clay (CC); MARCH 2, Polish song and dance company; MARCH 16, Timmy's Easter Parade Of Stars; APRIL 25, Leafs blank Red Wings 4-0 in Game 7 of Cup final; MAY 2, Greek community church service; MAY 3, Memorial Cup final, Marlboros def. Edmonton; MAY 12-15, Lipizzaner Stallions; MAY 16, Estonian Festival; MAY 27-31, Ringling Bros., Barnum and Bailey Circus; JUNE 7-11, Rotary International convention; JULY 8-11, Lion's club convention; SEPT. 7, Beatles (two shows); SEPT. 27, Mina and Pargi; SEPT. 29- OCT. 4, Wonderful World of Sports; OCT. 5; Jim Smith lacrosse benefit; OCT. 8, Ireland on Parade; OCT. 10, Leafs lose 3-2 to NHL all-stars; OCT. 17, 1964-65 home opener, Leafs 7, Boston 2; OCT. 25, Rita Pavone; OCT. 29, Irish military tattoo, NOV. 1, Gerry and the Pacemakers; NOV. 2, Dave Clark Five; NOV. 22- 27, Canadian rodeo; DEC. 1-8, Ice Capades; DEC. 13, Russia - Canada exhibition hockey.

65

LEAFS DRESSING ROOM

Former coach Mike Murphy has brought guests to the Gardens for four decades and no part of the tour has the kind of spine-tingling effects as walking through the clubhouse door.

"The first thing they want to know is where George Armstrong or Johnny Bower sat," said Murphy, who admits that's exactly what he did when he started playing for the Jr. A Marlies in the late 1960s.

Its location hasn't changed from the east side in 68 years, though a wall was torn down a few years ago to give the players more room. It now holds 30 stalls, with a weight training area and fitness facilities

built underneath the Hot Stove Lounge.

Under Murphy, a campaign to restore some of the room's prestige was launched in the summer of 1996. Plaques of Hall Of Fame Leafs now give players pause for thought, while Murphy put a mural of the evolving Leafs logo at the entrance.

The crowning touch was Conn Smythe's famous saying "Defeat Does Not Rest Lightly On Their Shoulders" highlighted on the wall at the back of the room.

The Leafs have given up their quarters only twice in team history, for Bob Hope and for Frank Sinatra.

Room at the top: The Leafs' dressing room has changed through the years as well as the mottos, but it remains a hallowed place today. (The Toronto Sun)

66

BOWER/BRODA BANNERS

Turk Broda gave only one piece of advice to Johnny Bower in their first meeting.

"He shook my hand, welcomed me to Toronto and told me, "always be proud to wear the Maple Leaf sweater," Bower recalled fondly. "It was the perfect thing to say."

That was 1959, when Broda—retired from playing goal with five Stanley Cups to his name—was coaching the Toronto Marlboros juniors at the Gardens.

Bower, a very late bloomer in the NHL in his mid 30s, took the words to heart and went on to help the Leafs to four Cups in the 1960s.

The link was completed in 1996 when banners honoring the No. 1 of both men were raised. Broda, who died in 1972, was represented at the ceremony by his ex-wife Betty and former Leaf Bob Davidson.

"I never saw Broda play, but George Armstrong told me he was a great money goaltender," Bower said.

Bower never strayed far from the Gardens after his retirement in 1970. He was a scout until the early 1990s, influencing many prospects.

"I used to wonder if I'd get my number up there," Bower said with a laugh.

"Armstrong said they'd probably hang me up there by my neck."

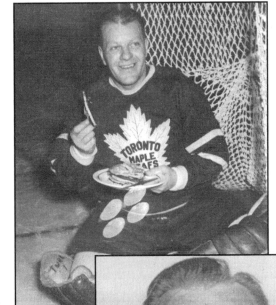

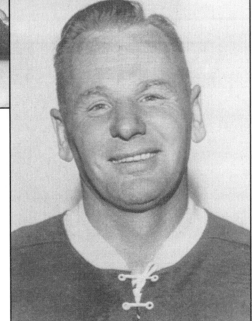

Turk Broda (top) and Johnny Bower (bottom)
(The Toronto Sun)

67

INDOOR TRACK AND FIELD

Hockey is a fast sport on blades, but the world's fastest runners, jumpers and throwers made news at the Gardens as well.

It began with the smash hit Telegram-Maple Leaf Indoor Games on January 25, 1963.

Bruce Kidd of the University of Toronto christened the $25,000 track by lapping the field and setting a Canadian record in the three-mile race. Nancy McCredie of Brampton also set a women's shot put mark, and American Dave Tork established a world indoor record in pole vault.

The Games continued until the 1980s, with sponsorship assumed by the Toronto Star. Canadian stars at the meets included Kidd, Bill Crothers, Harry Jerome, Abby Hoffman, Debbie Brill, Diane Jones and Debbie van Kiekebelt.

Gardens Events—1965

JAN. 3; wrestling; JAN. 5-8; curling; JAN. 10, Canada - Czechoslovakia exhibition hockey; JAN. 29, Telegram/Maple Leaf indoor games; FEB. 1, boxing, Patterson - Chuvalo (CC); FEB. 11, wrestling; FEB. 28, Canada - NHL oldtimers exhibition; MARCH 12, World figure skating tour; MARCH 14, Rita Pavone; MARCH 18, Claudio Villa; APRIL 24, Greek community church service; APRIL 25, Rolling Stones; MAY 2-8, Six-day bicycle races; MAY 11-13, Moiseyev ballet; MAY 16, International Variety Show; MAY 23, Italian Variety Show; MAY 25, boxing, Muhammad Ali vs. Liston (CC); MAY 29-30, Latvian song festival; JUNE 2-6, Ringling Bros., Barnum and Bailey circus; JUNE 8-10, ballet with Rudolf Nureyev; JULY 2-4, Alcoholics Anonymous convention; AUG. 17, The Beatles (two shows); Sept. 5, Beach Boys/Sonny and Cher; SEPT. 18-19, Royal Marines Tattoo; OCT. 22, USA vs. USSR volleyball; OCT. 23, 1965-66 home opener, Chicago 4, Leafs 0; OCT. 31, Rolling Stones; NOV. 1, boxing, Chuvalo vs. Ernie Terrell;NOV. 4, NDP convention; NOV. 22, boxing, Ali vs. Patterson (CC); DEC. 7-12, Ice Capades; DEC. 14, Russia - Marlboros exhibition.

68

TENNIS

Tennis was one of the first outdoor sports to take root at the Gardens, starting with the Bill Tilden touring exhibition in 1933. Tilden's 1941 show included American Alice Marble and Britain's Mary Hardwicke, the first two female athletes ever to compete at the Gardens.

Stars such as Don Budge, Bobby Riggs and Pancho Gonzales headlined through the years, but the sport's most successful years at the Gardens were unquestionably the 1980s.

Jimmy Connors and Ilie Nastase, wearing a Leafs and Canadiens jersey respectively, played a special exhibition match, followed in later years by big-purse tournaments that included John McEnroe, Bjorn Borg, Ivan Lendl, Yannick Noah and Vitas Gerulaitis.

Tennis Menace: Ilie Nastase imitating a victorious Bjorn Borg after winning a set at the Molson Tennis Challenge. (The Toronto Sun)

69

CLYDE GRAY/JOSE NAPOLES FIGHT
World Welterweight title fight, Sept. 22, 1973

Canada's Gray electrified the city by taking the Commonwealth title from Ghana's Eddie Blay at the Gardens earlier in the year, setting up the title shot with the powerful Mexican Napoles. Muhammad Ali and Howard Cosell handled a live telecast of the fight for ABC.

Though six years younger than the 33-year-old Napoles, Gray didn't use his speed advantage and found himself needing a knockout to win after 13 rounds. Gray's corner had the advantage of seeing the round-by-round scoring on the Gardens message board, which the visitor was unaware of. But Gray, bothered by a bit of blood that dripped into his left eye and a brief fifth-round knockdown, still couldn't touch his foe until he landed some rights to the jaw in the 15th.

"I started too slow," Gray said with a sigh after the Mexican and Canadian judges joined American referee Jay Edson in awarding Napoles a unanimous decision.

Dreams Dashed: Clyde Gray is consoled by manager Irv Ungerman after losing the World Welterweight title bout to Jose Napoles. (Peter Gill/The Toronto Sun)

Gardens Events—1966

JAN. 5, Sweden - Marlboros exhibition; JAN. 9, Czechoslovakia - Canada exhibition; JAN. 11-14, curling; JAN. 30, wrestling; FEB. 1-6, Ice Follies; FEB. 20-22, Hungarian Dance Company; FEB. 23, Toronto Symphony; FEB. 25, Telegram/Maple Leaf Indoor Games; MARCH 6, Rochester - Hershey AHL hockey; MARCH 29, boxing, Ali def. Chuvalo; APRIL 9, Greek community church service; MAY 4, Memorial Cup playoffs, Oshawa vs. Edmonton; MAY 8, Johnny Morandi; MAY 30, Indianapolis 500 (CC); JUNE 29, Rolling Stones; AUG. 17, The Beatles; SEPT. 24, The Toronto Sound; OCT. 1, Polish religious celebration; Oct 22, 1966-67 season opener, Leafs 4, Rangers 4; NOV. 6-7 Ukrainian Dance Company; NOV. 8-13, Ice Capades; NOV. 14, boxing, Ali vs. Cleveland Williams (CC); NOV. 17, wrestling; NOV.20, Beach Boys; NOV. 24-25, Royal Highland Fusiliers; DEC. 28, Czechoslovakia - Canadian Jr. all-stars exhibition.

BLIZZARD INDOOR SOCCER

When Toronto's North American Soccer League team took its act indoors at the Garden, even the players had doubts.

"I can still hear a couple of Scottish players looking around and going 'aauuuchhh, no'," Pat Surphlis, former media relations director for the Blizzard, said with a laugh. "Older players thought soccer on real grass was religion, and after putting up with Astroturf at the CNE, and now glass and boards at the Gardens, it was all too insulting.

"But the more we played, the more it caught on with the fans. Smaller, quick players such as David Byrne did well indoors. We drew 11,000 to some games."

It was a rough start for the Blizzard, which refused to

pay Harold Ballard's fee for TV lights and thus played in a dingy atmosphere. The cheap carpet often came apart and players suffered shin splints and rug burns.

"At first, some guys would fire the ball off the boards and not be ready when it would come back and hit them in the head," Surphlis said. "If a shot went high, our goalie would stand up and relax because he was used to it going in the crowd. Here, the ball could come back, hit him and go in.

The scores could get up over 20 goals, but people got into the action."

Soccer Power: The Toronto Blizzard indoor team at the Gardens had a brief but colorful history. (Pat Surphlis)

Gardens Events—1967

JAN. 10, Canada - Russia hockey exhibition; JAN. 31 -FEB. 5, Ice Follies; FEB. 6, boxing, Ali vs. Terrell (CC); FEB. 21, Toronto Police concert; FEB. 24, Telegram/Maple Leaf indoor games; MARCH 4, Terry Sawchuk's 100th career shutout; MARCH 9, Toronto - Detroit oldtimers hockey; APRIL 2, The Monkees; APRIL 9, Andy Williams/Henry Mancini; APRIL 29, Greek community church service; MAY 2, Leafs win Stanley Cup with 3-1 win over Montreal; MAY 16, Ontario Folk Arts Festival; MAY 22, Centennial Cool-Out, featuring The Guess Who; JULY 1, Mamas and the Papas; AUG. 2, Israeli Philharmonic; AUG. 9, Herman's Hermits; AUG. 13-19, Bolshoi Ballet; AUG. 20, Herb Alpert; SEPT. 7-9, Progressive Conservative Convention; SEPT. 17, Dominico Modugno; SEPT. 19, Telephone Pioneers of America; SEPT.26-OCT. 1, Moscow circus; OCT. 8, Italian Show; OCT. 13-15, Welsh and Scots Guard bands; OCT. 14, 1967-68 home opener, Leafs 5, Chicago 1; OCT. 27, United Appeal; OCT. 29, Italian variety show; NOV. 6-12, Ice Capades; NOV. 19, James Brown.

SHIP SHAPE

Legend has it that Conn Smythe brought in two cats to the new Gardens, to have the run of the building to keep it mouse-free.

It's also said he hired two painters whose job it was to cover even the slightest crack or chip so the building always looked brand new.

"Spit and polish was his trademark," said Brian Conacher, former vice-president of building operations. "That tradition has always continued. Mr. Ballard always made sure there was a fresh

coat of paint on the walls and Mr. Stavro spent a lot of time maintaining the history of the building and improving the aesthetics."

George Armstrong played more games than any other Leaf and called the Gardens the cleanest hockey building he's ever seen, despite its age.

"You went to some of the others (Boston Garden, Chicago Stadium) and it was just terrible," he said. "They were built at the same time and they became just dives."

Gardens Gallery • Garden's Super-Men

Conn Smythe could pick horses and hockey players and for an operation as complicated as the Gardens, he showed a talent for choosing innovative building superintendents. Doug Morris and Don (Shanty) MacKenzie combined to run the building from opening night until the dawn of the 1990s. Morris's long list of inventions includes hockey's first ice-re-surfacing machine, penalty clocks and implementation of the Gardens escalators, the first in a sports arena. Morris created the stage for the Metropolitan Opera's great shows at the Gardens in the 1950s and sang his own arias to test the sound. MacKenzie was a sergeant major with Conn Smythe's battery in France in 1945 when the latter offered him the post of assistant superintendent. At the urging of legendary Tely and Sun columnist Ted Reeve, who overheard the offer, MacKenzie accepted and eventually took over from Morris in the mid 1960s. Among MacKenzie's varied duties were recording the first game films for the Leafs, with a 16 mm Bolex camera, with film rushed across the street after the game for development, in time for morning viewing by the coach. MacKenzie was fortunate enough to capture the Bill Barilko 1951-Cup winning goal on film. He also calmed a nervous Pat Boone before a 1957 concert by tossing a baseball with him.

GARDENS INNOVATIONS

Here's a full list of advances in hockey technology that were first introduced at the Gardens, compiled by Leafs historian Andrew Podnieks:

Four-faced time clock, penalty clock, ice surfacing, painting the ice background white, red/blue lights, goal judge, timer for last-second goals, clocking player ice times, Herculite glass above the boards, arborite boards, separate penalty boxes and escalators.

Doug Morris, the Gardens' first superintendent and a great innovator for the building.

Gardens Gallery • Jobs for Life

Conn Smythe didn't forget the men who served under him in World War II. Many members of the 30th Sportsmen's battery were given jobs at the Gardens in peacetime or were set up at Smythe's sand and gravel company. It was also not uncommon to see members of the Memorial Cup champion Marlboros such as Bruce Boudreau, Bob Dailey, Mark Napier and John Anderson pushing brooms around the Gardens during the day, with school playing a less important role in those days. Another group who found refuge and work at the Gardens were some of Harold Ballard's acquaintances from his jail term at Kingston in the early 1970s.

73

HARLEM GLOBETROTTERS

When Sweet Georgia Brown whistled through the Gardens every spring, fans came out in droves.

The Harlem Globetrotters, the clown princes of basketball, delighted audiences of all ages for 70 years, with gravity-defying shots, passing and dribbling and at least one bucket of feathers in the face. The Trotters and their long-suffering opponents, the Washington Generals, often would play two Gardens shows as part of an annual world tour that often drew more than three million total spectators.

Meadowlark Lemon, Sweet Lou Dunbar and Lynette Woodward, the first female Trotter, never failed to disappoint, no matter how hard life was in many of the places they played.

"A troubled world is where we can do the most good," former Trotters front man Bobby Milton said prior to a Gardens visit in 1982.

Harlem Hi-Jinks: The Globetrotters never failed to make the Gardens laugh. (Hugh Wesley/The Toronto Sun)

Gardens Events—1968

JAN. 7, Canada - Italy hockey exhibition; JAN. 16, Leafs beat NHL all-stars 4-3; JAN. 21, Italian variety show; JAN. 30-FEB. 11, Ice Follies; MARCH 1, Telegram/Maple Leaf indoor games; MARCH 4, boxing'10(CC); MARCH 5, Buffalo Philharmonic; MARCH 10, Alfred Tucci; MARCH 17; Vera Lynn and British Revue; APRIL 7, James Brown; APRIL 19, Calypso Festival; APRIL 20, Greek community church service; APRIL 21, Leafs - Canadiens oldtimers game; MAY 1-5, Soviet Navy Ensemble; MAY 11, Italian variety show; MAY 8, Pro lacrosse, Toronto vs. Detroit; JUNE 30-JULY 3, Kiwanis convention; JULY 14,wrestling; SEPT. 9, Ford motors display; OCT. 4, British Variety Show; OCT. 16, 1968-69, home opener, Leafs tie Penguins 2-2, Jim Dorey sets single game penalty record; OCT. 27, Italian Variety Show; NOV. 1; Young Rascals/Union Gap; NOV. 4-11, Ice Capades; NOV. 15, James Brown.

74

WRESTLING IN THE '80s AND '90s

An astute combination of rock and roll and Hollywood glitz helped push the Gardens to the forefront of a North American wrestling boom. It was selling more of the sizzle than the steak, but 18,000 were cramming the Gardens every two weeks, close to violating the fire codes, in what Jack Tunney called "once in a lifetime business".

Frank Tunney died in 1983, and the next year Jack made a deal with the WWF. It featured former NWA stars such as Rowdy Roddy Piper and Paul Orndorff, along with two emerging headliners, Hulk Hogan and Randy (Macho Man) Savage.

The Wrestlemania series was just taking off in large outdoor venues in October 1985 when Hogan and Savage returned to the Gardens for a classic battle that sold out in two hours. Savage's wife/manager Miss Elizabeth, even received permission to use the sacred Gardens directors' lounge as a dressing room.

Hogan, Piper, Bret Hart, Lex Luger, Undertaker and the Ultimate Warrior continued to wrestle at the Gardens in the 1990s, but after the popular Hogan reduced his schedule the crowds started to fade. Tunney retired, cards were cut back to every two or three months and attendance dipped to just a few thousand.

Rowdy Roddy Piper was on the ropes as Ric Flair fed him the turnbuckle, but Piper and Hulk Hogan eventually won. (Stan Behal/Toronto Sun)

75

GORDIE DRILLON'S SCORING TITLE

There is something about the Maritimes and prolific Leaf scorers that clicks. Errol Thompson of Summeride P.E.I. was the left winger on a potent line with Darryl Sittler and Lanny McDonald, while fellow Islander Rick Vaive was the first Leaf to score 50 goals in one season. But the last Leaf to get his name on the Art Ross trophy is Moncton, N.B.'s Gordie Drillon.

The right winger's 26 goals and 26 assists were two points ahead of teammate Syl Apps in the 1937-38 season. Gaye Stewart came second to Chicago's Max Bentley in 1945-46, but no other Leaf has won the scoring title prior to 1998-99.

Drillon had been honored halfway through his big year by the mayor of Moncton, who presented him with a gold watch prior to a game against Chicago on January 8, 1938. The Leafs were shut out that night, but Drillon went on to get 294 points in 311 games, win a Cup and become the first Maritimer to be elected to the Hall Of Fame.

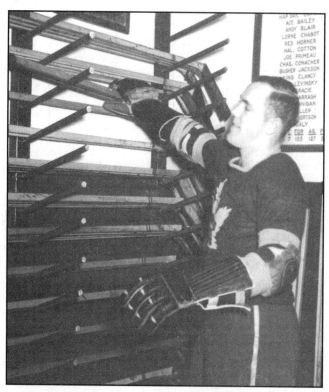

Maritime Sniper: Gordie Drillon, the Leafs' last scoring champ picks out his lumber. (The Toronto Sun)

Gardens Events—1969

JAN. 19, Canada - Russia hockey exhibition; JAN. 21 - FEB. 2, Ice Follies; FEB. 14, Telegram/Maple Leaf Indoor Games; MARCH 21, The Doors; MARCH 23, world figure skating show; MARCH 28, 48th Highlanders; APRIL 12, Greek community church service; APRIL 27, Paul Mauriat Orchestra; MAY 3, Jimi Hendrix Experience; MAY 7-11, Russian Festival; JUNE 12-13, International Floor Hockey; JUNE 15, Concert For Timmy; JUNE 20, James Brown; OCT. 2-4, British Tattoo; OCT. 6, Canadian - Italian boxing tourney; OCT. 12, Rita Pavone; OCT. 15, 1969-70 home opener, Leafs tie Montreal 2-2; OCT. 26, Italian Variety Show; OCT. 30, Herb Alpert; NOV. 3-9 Ice Capades; NOV. 10, Johnny Cash; NOV. 16, Vera Lynn; NOV. 28, Englebert Humperdinck; DEC. 4-5,7; Osipov Balalaika Orchestra; DEC. 26, Canada - Russia hockey exhibition.

76

CONCERT STORIES

Great music abounded at the Gardens, so did some great stories.

Record company big shots who were looking forward to meeting Bruce Springsteen in the Hot Stove after a concert, instead were treated to a steady parade of street people and handicapped beggars coming through the door. Apparently during a sightseeing jaunt along Yonge St. before the show, Springsteen invited everyone who looked downtrodden to come to the party.

The Rolling Stones almost were rejected by the Gardens in their first appearance in 1965, because someone pointed out how poorly they'd drawn in their U.S. tour the previous year.

Chicago was late by 4½

Gathering No Moss: Lineup for Rolling Stones tickets in 1972. (Jim Cowan/The Toronto Sun)

hours for one evening show because of trouble with their equipment at the U.S. border.

"It tells you a lot about Toronto audiences that almost everyone stayed until they came on," *Sun* entertainment editor Bob Thompson said.

Some of Alice Cooper's band's equipment was stolen, though he still went on. Elvis Presley smacked himself in the eye with a microphone and when John Bonham of Led Zeppelin launched into a long drum solo, other members of the band put their coats on and went outside in search of refreshments.

When straight-laced headliners Earth, Wind and Fire didn't like comedian Howie Mandel's salty jokes, they cut his microphone.

Gardens Events—1970

JAN. 1, Canada - Czechoslovakia hockey exhibition; JAN. 20-FEB. 1, Ice Follies; FEB. 5, Telegram/Maple Leaf indoor games; FEB. 16, boxing, Joe Frasier beats Jimmy Ellis (CC); MARCH 1, Buck Owens; MARCH 6, Arthur Fielder/Toronto Symphony; MARCH 13, England, Ireland, Scotland concert; MARCH 19-30, Disney on Parade; APRIL 3, Delaney and Bonnie and Friends; APRIL 25, Greek community church service; MAY 3, Ontario Teachers meeting; MAY 10, Wrestling; MAY 15-18, Garden Bros. circus; JUNE 1-7, Red Army music show; JUNE 11, Tom Jones; JUNE 14, World Cup soccer, Italy vs. Brazil (CC); JUNE 28-30, Moiseyev Dance Company; JULY 4, Latvian Song Festival; JULY 31, Caribana Extravaganza; AUG. 4, boxing, George Foreman def. Chuvalo (CC); SEPT. 19, Creedence Clearwater Revival; SEPT. 26-27, Coldstream Guards/Black Watch bands; OCT. 4, Sly and the Family Stone; OCT. 6-12, Moscow Circus on ice; OCT. 14, 1970-71 home opener, Leafs 7, St. Louis 3; OCT. 16, Blood, Sweat and Tears; OCT. 26, Boxing, Ali def. Jerry Quarry (CC); NOV. 3-8, Ice Capades; NOV. 26-27,29: Lipizzan Stallions; DEC. 7, boxing, Ali beats Oscar Bonavena (CC); DEC. 28, University hockey tourney.

HOT STOVE

.M. Pasmore, an ad executive with McLaren's, was the man who in 1931 christened Foster Hewitt's booth the "gondola" for its resemblance to an airship's gondola. He also created radio's Hot Stove League in 1939, the first ever broadcast intermission feature, that began in a cubbyhole adjacent to the Leafs dressing room.

The early lineup included Wes McKnight of CFRB, writers Bobby Hewitson of the *Telegram* and Elmer Ferguson, with host Court Benson and ex-Leaf Baldy Cotton.

In his book, *The Boys Of Saturday Night*, Scott Young said the group was at first forbidden to stray from a script, since World War II was raging and any mention of life beyond the Gardens, such as a party for a returning soldier, was a security risk.

But the group still produced an entertaining, off-the-cuff show that was as much a part of the broadcasts as Hewitt's play-by-play. The first TV version of the Hot Stove, had an actual stove in a studio about five minutes from the Gardens, but never equalled the popularity of its radio counterpart.

In 1963, the Hot Stove Club was opened on the Church St. side of the Gardens, the first private club in the NHL with 1,100 members today. The Leafs have used its four principal rooms to announce hirings, firings and signings, as well as host entertainment luminaries such as the Beatles and Bruce Springsteen.

Table Service: The Hot Stove is converted into a medical room for the 1979 training camp. (Bill Sanford/The Toronto Sun)

BEST OF THE BLUE AND WHITE

During the 1995-96 season, Gardens patrons were given the chance to vote for the greatest Leafs team in history.

In a clear indication of which age group makes up Leafs' fans, all five choices played after 1960. From a list of 19 finalists of all eras, the fans picked Johnny Bower in goal, Borje Salming and Tim Horton on defence, Frank Mahovlich on left wing, Lanny McDonald on the right and Darryl Sittler at centre.

Asked his opinion of the best Toronto Marlboro juniors he ever saw, longtime Dukes GM Frank Bonello pointed to members of the latter-day Memorial cup champions, such as forwards Mark Napier, Paulin Bordeleau, Steve Shutt, defenceman Mark Howe and goaltender Mike Palmateer. But he figured that Jim Gregory, whose 1965 team almost graduated to the NHL en masse, would make a good case for his players.

Great Leafs: The all-time Maple Leafs team was chosen by fans in 1996. Left to right: Johnny Bower, Lanny McDonald, Darryl Sittler and Frank Mahovlich. (Wanda Goodwin/The Toronto Sun)

Gardens Events,—1971

JAN. 14, NBA exhibition, Los Angeles vs. Cincinnati; JAN. 19-31, Ice Follies; FEB. 1, Chicago; FEB. 5, Telegram/Maple Leaf Indoor Games; FEB. 7, Mazowsze Polish music show; FEB. 11-12, Progressive Conservatives convention; FEB. 19, Toronto - Montreal oldtimers hockey; FEB. 26, Toronto Symphony; MARCH 7, roller derby; MARCH 8, boxing, Frazier beats Ali (CC); MAY 10, boxing, Chuvalo beats Jimmy Ellis; MAY 13-16, Garden Bros. circus; MAY 21-23, Georgia State Ensemble; MAY 24, filming of the movie Face Off; MAY 28, 48th Highlanders; MAY 29, Tom Jones; MAY 30, Sly and The Family Stone/James Gang/Buddy Miles; JUNE 4-6, antique show; JUNE 9-10, international floor hockey; AUG. 7-8 dog show; SEPT. 4, Led Zeppelin; OCT. 1-3, Lippizan Stallions; OCT. 9, Grand Funk Railroad; OCT. 10, Italian Variety Show; OCT. 13, 1971-72 home opener, Red Wings 5, Leafs 3; NOV. 2-7 Ice Capades; DEC. 2, NBA exhibition, Buffalo vs. Baltimore; DEC. 3, Ike and Tina Turner; DEC. 7, roller derby; DEC. 9, Rod Stewart and The Faces.

79

TREASURE TROVE

The Gardens proved to be an archaeological storehouse in 1990 when excavations for a new weight room under the Hot Stove Lounge yielded 19th century bottles, dishes and the lid of an ornate bed pan.

Collector pop and beer bottles from the 1920s and '30s are still discovered now and then in cubby holes and false ceilings used by the original workmen when they hid out on break. Not long ago, former building superintendent Wayne Gillespie found a piece of lumber inscribed "we are doing this at 11:30 p.m., Sept. 28, 1931."

Inside the engineering room, some of the original equipment has been bronzed as well as a drill press for tube skates, thought to belong to Harold Ballard's father who had a thriving machinist trade in the early 1900s.

Gardens Events—1972

JAN. 9, wrestling; JAN. 14, four-team ABA exhibition; JAN. 18-30, Ice Follies; FEB. 4, Maple Leaf indoor games; FEB. 13, Three Dog Night; FEB. 25, Toronto Symphony; MARCH 18, world figure skating show; MARCH 28, Moody Blues; APRIL 3, Timmy Tyke tournament; APRIL 5, Joe Cocker; APRIL 10, Regimental Band/Scots Guards; APRIL 19, soccer, Glasgow Celtic vs. Inter-Milan (CC); APRIL 21; Rock and Roll Revival with Little Richard/Gary U.S. Bonds/Coasters; APRIL 29, two European Cup soccer games (CC); MAY 13, two European Cup soccer games (CC); MAY 31, soccer, Ajax vs. Inter Milan (CC); JUNE 4, Jethro Tull; JUNE 26, Edgar Winter/Humble Pie; JULY 15, Rolling Stones/Stevie Wonder; AUG. 22, Team Canada inter-squad game; SEPT. 4, Canada beats Russia 4-1 in Game 2 of summit series; SEPT. 7, Rod Stewart and The Faces; SEPT. 19, United Appeal gala; SEPT. 26, Ten Years After/Edgar Winter/Peter Frampton; SEPT. 28, Dukla Ukrainian Dance Company; OCT. 5, Elton John; OCT. 6, roller derby; OCT. 7, 1972-73 home opener, Chicago 3, Leafs 1; OCT. 8, Festival Italiano; OCT. 17, Liberal party rally; OCT. 20, Rock and Roll Revival; OCT. 27, roller derby; OCT. 31, Yes/J. Geils Band; NOV. 3, Carabinieri band; NOV. 8-13, Ice Capades; NOV. 21, boxing, live and on closed circuit; DEC. 29, Czechoslovakia - Russia exhibition hockey.

Gardens Gallery • Safe and Sound

Though many priceless hockey artifacts were trashed by Harold Ballard, such as Foster Hewitt's gondola and Cup banners which met their end as drop cloths for painters, some workers rescued items of significance, such as pictures and programs.

"It was like hiding paintings from the Nazis," sound technician Jim McLean said jokingly. "Everyone has a real affection for this place."

Ballard sometimes did have a soft spot, calling the Hockey Hall of Fame the day before he junked a closet full of memorabilia. Director of acquisitions Phil Pritchard made it to the Gardens with his truck in time to save massive scrap books that had decades of clippings and pictures.

Some things proved impossible to move, regardless of motive. The original Gardens safe is so heavy that renovations were carried on around it. There's also a wrought iron spiral staircase in the business office that looks like something out of a Hitchcock movie.

80

99-POINT YEAR IN '92-'93

When Peter Zezel fired a 2-1 overtime goal past Curtis Joseph, the Leafs capped their most successful regular season in club history.

Zezel's goal netted the club its 99th point and 25th Gardens victory, both records, though a loss in Chicago the next night denied them 100 points.

But the Leafs gained 32 points from the previous season, their biggest leap ever.

The Leafs went on to play three seven-game series in the playoffs, with coach

Pat Burns capturing the Jack Adams Trophy and Doug Gilmour the Frank Selke Trophy as top defensive forward.

Year to Remember: One of the happy moments for coach Pat Burns and the Leafs during their 99-point run in 1992-93.

CIRCUS

When locals talk of the circus at the Gardens, they usually referred to the hockey team in the 1970s and '80s.

But the real big top was a much anticipated event for all ages. The most famous circus troupes, Ringling Brothers, Barnum and Bailey, Shrine Circus, Garden Brothers and the Moscow Circus have been stopping by since the building opened. But there were some unusual moments...

In the 1960s, a tiger wandered out of its cage when a cleaner didn't close it properly.

"The guy came running down the hall shouting to Don McKenzie, 'the tiger is loose!, the tiger is loose!,' Paul Morris said with a laugh. "Don calmly advised him to close the office door."

The tiger went past the Zamboni where a frightened worker had clambered on top,

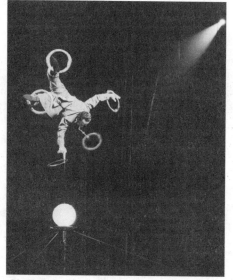

Big Top Gardens: The circus has long been a staple of the building. (Jim Kennedy/The Toronto Sun)

then sniffed at the door of a supervisor, who worked away oblivious to its presence.

"Had he opened his door, he'd have hit the tiger right in the head," Morris said.

On the floor behind the seats of the north end are some large steel rings anchored to the floor. These are used to keep elephants tied down during circus shows, but haven't always worked. One elephant momentarily got loose during a show in the 1950s, wrapped its trunk around a ceiling water pipe and crushed it.

As a Gardens worker grabbed a hose with the intent of scaring the elephant with a blast of water, he was halted just in time by the trainer. He was told had he turned the water on, he would've been crushed by the animal for certain.

Gardens Gallery • The Line of Fire

The Gardens penalty box, a second home to Leafs such as Tiger Williams and Tie Domi, used to be located between the player benches. The potential for mayhem was recognized in the 1940s, when the sin bin, the time keeper and penalty time keeper were moved across the ice.

82

ANIMALS, ANIMALS, ANIMALS

Through the years, four-legged creatures left their mark on the Gardens, if not an odor that lingered for a few days after.

The crowd favorites were not just the lions, tigers and elephants of that accompanied the circus. Greyhound racing was attempted in 1938, but ran into trouble when the mechanical rabbit wouldn't cooperate. A major dog show in 1971 attracted 700 owners and 1,000 breeds.

Horses always have been popular attractions, everything from the 29 white stallions of the Spanish Riding School of Vienna, to show jumping, to a horse that walked up and down from the greens to ice level to simulate climbing a mountain. Cowboy singers Roy Rogers and Gene Autrey brought their famous mounts Trigger and Champion to the building, but so many fans pulled at Trigger's tail that a fake one was attached. The Moscow Circus offered to pit its hockey-playing bears against the Leafs in the 1950s, but King Clancy refused for safety reasons. One night a squirrel got in the building and disrupted a game as it raced through the seats.

Animals were frequent visitors to the Gardens. (The Toronto Sun)

Gardens Gallery • No Horsesense

A Leafs home game has never had to be cancelled because of a building-related problem, but there have been a couple of close calls.

About 30 years go, some rodeo horses urinated through the dirt and plywood that covered the ice. When the underground pipes were turned back on to prepare for the next game, brown lumps appeared all over the ice surface and the game was delayed a hour, then played on brown ice.

83

THE METROPOLITAN OPERA

According to Stan Obodiac, the Gardens was the first arena in the world to produce opera back in October 1936 with productions of Aida and Faust. But Doug Morris' ingenuity led to successful endeavors by the famed Metropolitan Opera of New York, starting in 1952.

Morris noticed that the 90-foot beams he'd seen in the ceiling of a new Loblaws supermarket would be perfect to lay out a theatre grid, laid end to end with the seats rising from floor level to about six feet. Morris, a choir singer in his native England, sang his own arias on stage to test the sound.

The Met broke several attendance records while in Toronto and there was thought given to turning the Gardens into an opera house when the Leafs depart for the Air Canada Centre.

Opera crowd gathers in the Gardens lobby. (The Toronto Telegram)

Opera-tion: The Gardens is readied for the Metropolitan Opera. This was the first time an opera stage was built in a hockey venue.

84

LACROSSE

The traditional close ties between lacrosse and hockey date from the first ever game played at the Gardens on May 3, 1932. The Maple Leafs, members of the International Lacrosse League, borrowed Bucko McDonald from the hockey team and he scored in a 12-5 win over the Tecumsehs.

The Mann Cup, senior lacrosse's championship trophy, has been contested many times at the Gardens, starting in 1932 when the local Mimico Mountaineers beat the Squamish Indians and then Winnipeg to win the title. A new Toronto entry in the National Lacrosse League is planned for 1999, playing out of the Gardens.

Gardens Events 1973

JAN. 15, Neil Young; JAN. 16-28, Ice Follies; JAN. 22,boxing, Foreman def. Frazier (CC); JAN. 29, Toronto Indoor Soccer League games; FEB. 2, Maple Leaf Indoor Games; FEB. 5, TISL games; FEB. 12, boxing,Clyde Gray def. Eddie Blay; FEB. 20, Santana; FEB. 25, Mazowsze Dance Company; MARCH 2, Toronto Symphony; MARCH 11, Pink Floyd; MARCH 30, Liza Minelli/Desi Arnaz, Jr./celebrity tennis; MAY 5, Marlies - Peterborough junior attendance record of almost 17,000; APRIL 1, Festival Italiano; APRIL 2, Timmy Tyke tournament; APRIL 10, World Hockey Association playoffs, Ottawa vs. New England; APRIL 13, Paul Butterfield/Wet Willie; MAY 4, Frank Zappa; MAY 6, Ukrainian Catholic Council; MAY 11, Professional indoor track; MAY 19, Rock and Roll Revival with Bill Haley/Dion/Fabian/Chiffons; MAY 26, roller derby; MAY 30, Jethro Tull; JUNE 8, The Donna Fargo Show; JUNE 24, wrestling; JUNE 28, British rock show with Herman's Hermits, Pacemakers and Billy J. Kramer; AUG. 13-24, GM car show; AUG. 29, Carlos Santana; SEPT. 10, boxing,, Ali def. Ken Norton (CC); SEPT. 22, boxing, Jose Napoles def. Gray; SEPT. 23, wrestling; OCT. 4, NBA, Buffalo vs. Milwaukee; OCT. 5, roller derby; OCT. 7, Festival Italiano; OCT. 10, 1973-74 home opener, Leafs 7, Buffalo 4; OCT. 11, boxing; OCT. 21, roller derby; OCT. 26, NBA, Buffalo vs. Cleveland; NOV. 2, Johnny Cash; NOV. 4, Ukrainian World Congress/NBA, Buffalo vs. Chicago: NOV. 5, Edgar Winter; NOV. 6, roller derby; NOV. 13-18, Ice Capades; DEC. 5, roller derby; DEC. 7, Emerson, Lake and Palmer; DEC. 9, NBA, Buffalo vs. Boston; DEC. 10, Siberian Dance Ensemble; DEC. 14, Alice Cooper; DEC. 16, Whipper Watson's Skate For Timmy; DEC. 23, NBA, Buffalo vs. Washington; DEC. 27, Leafs open practice; DEC. 31, Winter Pop with Seals and Crofts/Crowbar/Stampeders.

Gardens Events—1974

JAN. 1, CCM hockey tournament; JAN. 6, NBA, Buffalo vs. Atlanta; JAN. 10, Bob Dylan and The Band; JAN. 15-27, Ice Follies; JAN. 28, boxing, Ali def. Frazier (CC); FEB. 3, basketball exhibition, Israel vs. U of Waterloo/NBA, Buffalo vs. Philadelphia; FEB. 7, indoor soccer, NASL'10all-stars vs. Red Army; FEB. 8, roller derby; FEB. 13, World Cup soccer, Spain vs. Yugoslavia (CC); FEB. 15, Maple Leaf indoor games; FEB. 18, boxing, Gray def. Bunny Grant; FEB. 22, Yes; FEB. 26, World Cup soccer, West Germany v Italy (CC); MARCH 1, Toronto Symphony; MARCH 11, Johnny Winter; MARCH 12, Big Band Cavalcade; MARCH 13, volleyball, Canada vs. Japan, Korea; MARCH 16, roller derby; MARCH 19-24, Peter Pan; MARCH 26, boxing, Foreman def. Norman (CC); APRIL 5, The Guess Who; APRIL 7, WHA playoffs, Toronto Toros vs. Cleveland; MAY 3-4, screening of A Time To Run; MAY 21, lacrosse, Toronto vs. Quebec; MAY 24-25, International floor hockey; JUNE 12, gymnastics, Canada vs. Russia; JUNE 13-16, 18; JULY 3, 19, 22-23, World Cup soccer (CC); JUNE 17, boxing, live and closed circuit; JUNE 26, international basketball tourney; JULY 21, Tae-Kwon-Do exhibition; AUG. 21-30, GM car show; SEPT. 8, Evel Knievel's Snake River Canyon jump (CC); SEPT. 10-15, Ukrainian Festival On Ice; SEPT. 19, Canada - Russia hockey exhibition; SEPT. 26, NBA, Buffalo vs. Detroit; SEPT. 28, Welsh Guards and the Argyll and Sutherland Highlanders; SEPT. 29 Slask, Polish dance company; OCT. 2, Eric Clapton; OCT. 7, Rick Wakeman; OCT. 9, 1974-75 home opener, Leafs def. Kansas City Scouts 6-2; OCT. 15, Toros open WHA season vs. New England; OCT. 21, Van Morrison; OCT. 29, boxing, Ali def. Foreman (CC); OCT. 30, roller derby; NOV. 5, world gymnastics meet; NOV. 7-17, Ice Capades; NOV. 18, Elton John; DEC. 6, George Harrison/Ravi Shankar; DEC. 16, Genesis; DEC. 20, Whipper Watson's Skate for Timmy; DEC. 26, Marlboros vs. Czechoslovakia hockey exhibition.

PRESS BOX

The Hockey Hall of Fame members who've populated the Gardens since 1931 didn't all toil on the ice, behind the bench or in the executive offices.

The press box has been home to 11 Toronto sports writers who are in the Hall's media wing, along with broadcasters Foster Hewitt, Wes McKnight—and Howie Meeker.

The scribes include Red Burnett, Jim Coleman, Milt Dunnell, Trent Frayne, George Gross, Rex MacLeod, Frank Orr, Jim Proudfoot, Al Strachan, Jim Vipond and Scott Young.

The press box originally was situated in the South East corner reds and had room for 20 reporters and their clacking typewriters. The modern facility runs the length of the East side, with prime

seating for the four Toronto papers, the home and visiting radio crews and NHL statisticians.

The video replay booth and the Leafs' management box are at opposite ends of press row, while the TV broadcasts originate from the West box, which also includes the scoreboard operations crew.

During the 1993 playoffs, the press box capacity record was broken when staff from 25 newspapers, five magazines, 10 radio stations and 15 TV stations crowded in with the usual cast of scouts, injured players and visiting management.

The latter can get as worked up as the players on the ice. Excitable Blues' general manager Ron Caron was a classic example, once tossing a chair at public relations director Bob Stellick and challenging him to a fight.

Gardens Events—1975

JAN. 2, Marlboros vs. Russia hockey exhibition; JAN. 14-26, Ice Follies; JAN. 27, J. Geils Band; FEB. 6, Marvin Gaye/Ike and Tina Turner; FEB. 9, Marlboros vs. Japanese national team; FEB. 14; Maple Leaf indoor games; FEB. 28, Toronto Symphony; MARCH 18, Stevie Wonder; MARCH 29, world figure skating tour; MARCH 31, Timmy Tyke, tournament; APRIL 3, Johnny Winter; APRIL 8, Leafs playoff game in Los Angeles (CC); APRIL 11, Jehovah's Witnesses; APRIL 23, John Denver; APRIL 26, boxing, Foreman Vs. Five, (CC); MAY 2, Alice Cooper; MAY 10, Frank Sinatra (two shows); MAY 17, Latamukesh Show; JUNE 17-18, Rolling Stones; JUNE 30, boxing, Ali def. Joe Bugner (CC); JULY 19, Yes; JULY 21, international women's volleyball; AUG. 9, Todd Rundgren; AUG. 17, Olympic boxing teams, Canada vs. Russia; SEPT. 1, Jefferson Starship; SEPT. 5, Doobie Brothers; SEPT. 27, Olympic figure skating preview; SEPT. 29, Bee Gees; SEPT. 30, Ali def. Frazier, (CC); OCT. 7, Jethro Tull; OCT. 8, Festival Italiano; OCT. 11, 1975-76 home opener, Leafs 2, Chicago 1; OCT. 16, Rick Wakeman; OCT. 27, Rod Stewart and The Faces; NOV. 4, world gymnastics meet; NOV. 6-16, Ice Capades; NOV. 19, Isaac Hayes; DEC. 2, Rolling Thunder Review, with Bob Dylan, Joan Baez; DEC. 11, The Who; DEC. 18, Marlies vs. Moscow Selects; DEC. 23, Whipper Watson Christmas Skate For Timmy.

TEAM CANADA '74

In many ways, this was the high point of the World Hockey Association series with the Russian powerhouse. Again, it was the only game Canada would win at home, a chance for legends Gordie Howe and Bobby Hull to meet the Russians after they'd been left off the '72 team. Hull, vilified two years earlier by the NHL, basked in the introductory cheers.

Canada had almost beaten the Russians in the Quebec City opener, a 3-3 tie, and this 4-1 win looked to put the stamp of approval on the calibre of the upstart league.

Gordie and son Mark both assisted on Ralph Backstrom's opening goal. Hull made it 3-1 early in the third and assisted on another, though the game always will be remembered for a disallowed Russian goal despite plenty of evidence the puck was in under Gerry Cheevers' crossbar.

Gardens Events—1976

JAN. 9, ZZ Top; JAN. 13-25, Ice Follies; FEB. 3, Mazowsze Polish Dance Company; FEB. 7, Darryl Sittler's record 10-point game; FEB. 13, Maple Leaf Indoor Games; MARCH 5, Toronto Symphony/Police choir; MARCH 14, Royal Marines/Black Watch band; MARCH 30, Timmy Tyke; APRIL 1, Genesis; APRIL 3, Darryl Sittler first Leaf to 100 points; APRIL 11, Festival Di Primavera; APRIL 18, Bad Company/Styx; APRIL 20, Supertramp; APRIL 22, Sittler's record five-goal playoff game; APRIL 24, Lippizaner Stallions; APRIL 26, KISS; MAY 1, Frank Sinatra; MAY 9, Paul McCartney and Wings; MAY 10, Joe Cocker; MAY 13, Johnny Winter; MAY 27, Santana; MAY 28, soccer, England vs. Italy (CC); JUNE 11, Olympic benefit concert with Gordon Lightfoot, Liona Boyd; JUNE 15, boxing, Foreman def. Frazier (CC); JUNE 25, Ali vs. Antonio Inoki (CC); JULY 3-4, Latvian Song Festival; AUG. 8, wrestling; AUG. 11, Bay City Rollers; AUG. 13-14, roller skating; AUG. 18, Loggins and Messina; AUG. 23-29, GM 10car show; SEPT. 3, Canada Cup, Sweden beats USA; SEPT. 5, Canada Cup, Finland vs. Czechoslovakia; SEPT. 7, Canada Cup, Canada vs. Sweden; SEPT. 8-10, Ford car show; SEPT. 11, Canada Cup, Canada vs. USSR; SEPT. 13, Canada Cup playoff, Canada vs. Czechoslovakia; SEPT. 14, Electric Light Orchestra; SEPT. 16, Nazareth/Mahogany Rush; SEPT. 23-24, Toller Cranston Ice Show; SEPT. 1 28, boxing, Ali def. Norton (CC); OCT. 3, Kishore Kumar; OCT. 5, Jackson Browne; OCT. 10, Festival Italiano; OCT. 13, 1976-77 home opener, Leafs 7, Boston 5; OCT. 15, Jeff Beck; OCT. 19, Paul Anka; OCT. 21, The Who; OCT. 22, Neil Diamond; OCT. 25, Charlie Pride; NOV. 2, gymnastics; NOV. 4-14, Ice Capades; NOV. 15, Doobie Brothers; NOV. 16, Frank Zappa; NOV. 21, Italian variety show; NOV. 24, Equestrian grand prix; NOV. 29, Bee Gees; NOV. 30, Robin Trouer; DEC. 10, The Strawbs; DEC. 29, Skate For Timmy; DEC. 31, Rush.

Gardens Events—1977

JAN. 3, Rush; JAN. 16, Beach Boys; JAN. 18-30, Ice Follies; FEB. 1, Queen; FEB. 2, Defenceman Ian Turnbull's five-goal game; FEB. 6, wrestling; FEB. 11, Maple Leaf indoor games; FEB. 13, Bruce Springsteen; FEB. 22, Visit by Prince Andrew for private high school tournament; MARCH 3-4, tri-country track meet; MARCH 6, Genesis; MARCH 8, Santana; MARCH 22, Peter Gabriel; MARCH 24, Jethro Tull; MARCH 25, Catholic Youth Organization hockey; MARCH 30, Eagles; APRIL 4, ELO; APRIL 11, Timmy Tyke tournament; APRIL 18, Al Stewart; APRIL 24, Domenico Modugno; APRIL 29, The Kinks; MAY 1, Boston; MAY 6-8, Shrine circus; JUNE 1-2, Supertramp; JUNE 12, Ted Nugent/Uriah Heep; JUNE 16, Hall and Oates; JUNE 21, Blue Oyster Cult/Todd Rundgren; AUG. 9, Bob Marley; AUG. 15, Peter Frampton; AUG. 27, Ashe Bosle; SEPT. 4-18, GM car show; SEPT. 22, Toller Cranston's Ice Show; SEPT. 25, Mohamad Rafi and Party; SEPT. 29, Frank Zappa; SEPT. 30, Grenadier and Scots Guards bands; OCT. 2, Italian music show; OCT. 5-9, Moscow circus; OCT. 12, Rod Stewart; OCT. 15, 1977-78 home opener, Buffalo 5, Leafs 2; OCT. 24, Steve Miller; OCT. 30, Italian variety show; OCT. 31, Chicago; NOV. 1, international gymnastics; NOV. 3-13, Ice Capades; NOV. 21, Queen; NOV. 22, equestrian grand prix; NOV. 24, Gino Vanelli; DEC. 1, Billy Joel; DEC. 10, Aerosmith; DEC. 28, Skate For Timmy; DEC. 30, Rush

FIRST RUSSIAN VISITORS

The first sighting of a Russian on Gardens ice was November 22, 1957 when Moscow Dynamo took on the world amateur champion Whitby Dunlops. Despite laughably out-of-date equipment, the Russians led 2-0 in the first period.

"They passed the puck boom-boom-boom like robots," Toronto Marlboros GM Frank Bonello said. "There were 14,327 in the Gardens that night and you could've heard a pin drop. We settled down and won 7-2."

The Russians have had trouble at the Gardens ever since.

Gardens Events—1978

JAN. 2, Leafs vs. Kladno of Czechoslovakia; JAN. 5, Bob Hope; JAN. 17-29, Ice Follies; FEB. 2-3, Emerson, Lake and Palmer; FEB. 10, Maple Leaf indoor games; FEB. 16, Santana; MARCH 9, Blue Oyster Cult; MARCH 10, Tony Bennett; MARCH 17, Jimmy Buffett; MARCH 19, World figure skating tour; MARCH 21, Triumph; MARCH 26, Timmy Tyke tourney; APRIL 2-4, Shrine circus; APRIL 9, Eric Clapton; APRIL 12, The Tubes; MAY 1, David Bowie; MAY 3, Nazareth; MAY 20, Bob Seger; JUNE 3-4, Ontario floor hockey games; JUNE 9, Bob Marley; JUNE 11-14, Billy Graham Crusade; JUNE 17, Noor Jehan; JUNE 19, Ted Nugent; JULY 2, Lithuanian song festival; JULY 17, Crosby, Stills and Nash; JULY 25, Leo Sayer; JULY 30-31, Neil Diamond; AUG. 6, Kishore Kumar; AUG. 19, Linda Ronstadt; AUG. 21, Boston; SEPT. 19-22, Ford car show; OCT. 1, Neil Young; OCT. 3, Frank Zappa; OCT. 5, Billy Joel; OCT. 8, Festival Italiano; OCT. 12, Bob Dylan; OCT. 14, 1978-79 home opener, Leafs 10, Islanders 7; OCT. 15, Jethro Tull; OCT. 16, Peter Gabriel; OCT. 20, Donna Summer; NOV. 1, Al Stewart; NOV. 2-12, Ice Capades; NOV. 13, Grease concert; NOV. 14, international gymnastics; NOV. 16, Bruce Springsteen; NOV. 27, 10 CC; NOV. 30, Moody Blues; DEC. 3 Queen; DEC. 8, Bob Seeger; DEC. 17, Whipper Watson Night; DEC. 28-29, 31, Rush.

Gardens Gallery • The Plane Truth

Harold Ballard opposed the NHL-sponsored exhibition games with Russian club teams that began in the 1970s, refusing to involve the Leafs and the Gardens.

When Moscow Dynamo finally was allowed to come to the Gardens to play a Canadian amateur team in 1985, not long after the shooting down of a South Korean passenger jet, Ballard seized the opportunity to make a point.

In the last minute of play, he ordered the scoreboard to flash "Remember Korean Airlines Flight 007. Don't cheer, Just Boo. Harold." Russian officials were angry, but Ballard made his point.

88

USHERS/USHERETTES

As the Gardens entered its 67th season, the longest serving usher on a staff of almost 200 men and women is Dennis Goodwin, who started in 1949. Few people who worked the night Bill Barilko lit up the Gardens with his Cup-winning goal survived to punch tickets for heavy metal bands Metallica and Guns' n Roses.

"I think those concerts are when they started giving us older fellows earplugs," Goodwin said with a laugh. "The sound equipment they use today is incredible. I preferred Perry Como when he was here."

Goodwin was 16 when he was given the choice of selling Eskimo Pies in the seats or becoming an usher. Today, he's a fixture in the East greens, section 65-67, as well as being one of the Leafs' dressing room watch dogs. Ushers have enjoyed the most longevity among Gardens part-time employees, with Smythe and Harold Ballard often turning a blind eye to the mandatory retirement age.

"As long as you could breathe and walk in a straight line you were in," Goodwin said, recalling an old Gardens' wisecrack.

He was asked the biggest changes and crowd trends he's seen in the building since the '40s.

Girls in Blue: Gardens usherette uniforms in 1945. (The Toronto Sun)

"Crowd spontaneity," he said. "You never used to need a scoreboard to tell you to cheer like to-day."

The '67 Cup sticks out as Goodwin's hockey highlight, Elvis the most exhilarating of the concerts.

"People wanted to stand up in their seats for Elvis, and in those days it just wasn't done," he said. "But if you told them they had to sit, you were nice and they were polite, too.

"They've changed a bit since, not so much the hockey fans, but some people at the concerts. They started smoking that wacky tabacky and I've even seen 12-year-olds in the section try to sell it."

The usherette uniforms in 1972. (Dave Cooper/The Toronto Sun)

Gardens Events—1979

JAN. 16-28, Ice Follies; FEB. 2, Maple Leaf indoor games; MARCH 18, Santana/Eddie Money; MARCH 19, Trooper; MARCH 30, Harlem Globetrotters; APRIL 13, Timmy Tyke tourney; APRIL 20, Yes; APRIL 23, Village People; APRIL 25, Gino Vanelli; MAY 6-7, Rod Stewart; MAY 9, Liberal party rally; MAY 11, Toronto police concert; MAY 15, Van Halen; MAY 25-27, Garden Bros. Circus; JUNE 12, Cheap Trick; JUNE 14, Cars; JUNE 22, Max Webster; JUNE 28-JULY 4, Kiwanis convention; JULY 29, Steve Martin; AUG. 4, KISS; AUG. 25-26, Mormons conference; AUG. 31, The Bee Gees; SEPT. 9, wrestling; SEPT. 16-21, Leafs training camp; OCT. 5, Jethro Tull; OCT. 7, Abba; OCT. 10, 1979-80 home opener, Rangers 6, Leafs 3; OCT. 11, Earth, Wind and Fire; OCT. 12, Little River Band; OCT. 18-19, Styx; NOV. 1, Bob Marley; NOV. 6-11, Ice Capades.

Gardens Events—1980

JAN. 11, Aerosmith; JAN. 15-27, Ice Follies; FEB. 1 Maple Leaf indoor games; FEB. 22-24 Garden Bros. circus; MARCH 20, Marty Robbins/Hank Williams Jr.; MARCH 21, John Denver; MARCH 23; Toronto - Montreal oldtimers game; MARCH 29; Wayne Gretzky's first NHL game at the Gardens; APRIL 3, ZZ Top; APRIL 6, APRIL Wine, Johnny Winter; APRIL 23, pro tennis, Jimmy Connors vs. Ilie Nastase; APRIL 27, Beach Boys; MAY 5-6, The Who; JUNE 3, Nazareth; JUNE 16, Little River Band; JUNE 20, boxing, Roberto Duran def. Sugar Ray Leonard (CC); JUNE 21, Prism; JUNE 23-24, Genesis; JULY 3, Peter Gabriel; JULY 5-13, Baptist World Congress; JULY 7, Joan Armatrading; JULY 18, Van Halen; JULY 28, AC/DC and Streetheart; AUG. 6, Kenny Loggins; AUG. 7, Journey; AUG. 9, Cheap Trick; AUG. 29, Yes; SEPT. 5, Ted Nugent/Humble Pie; SEPT. 7, Elton John; SEPT. 21, Melody Queen, SEPT. 26, Triumph; SEPT. 28, Paul Simon; OCT. 2, boxing, Larry Holmes def. Ali (CC); OCT. 11, 1980-81 home opener, Rangers 8, Leafs 3; OCT. 19, wrestling; OCT. 24-26, World Cup gymnastics; NOV. 4-9, Ice Capades; NOV. 11, Frank Zappa; NOV. 16, wrestling; NOV. 20-21, Barry Manilow; NOV. 25, boxing, Duran vs. Leonard (CC); NOV. 27. Toronto Blizzard indoor soccer debuts with 7-4 win over Calgary; NOV. 30, Blizzard vs. Edmonton; DEC. 14, Blizzard vs. Calgary; DEC. 31, Max Webster.

Gardens Events—1981

JAN. 4, Blizzard v Calgary; JAN. 8, Blizzard vs. Vancouver; JAN. 18, Blizzard vs. Edmonton; JAN. 20-21, Bruce Springsteen; JAN. 22, Blizzard vs. Edmonton; JAN. 29, Blizzard vs. Edmonton; FEB. 4-8, Molson tennis; FEB. 9, Elvis Costello; FEB. 15, Blizzard vs. Vancouver; MARCH 6, Boomtown Rats; MARCH 17, Ted Nugent; MARCH 22-25, Rush; JUNE 6, Kenny Rogers; JUNE 25, Astrowars; JUNE 30, Santana; JULY 17, The Tubes; JULY 22, Tom Petty; JULY 27, Ozzie Osbourne; AUG. 4, Van Halen; AUG. 7-8, Styx; SEPT. 9, Pat Benetar; SEPT. 25, Kinks; OCT. 10, 1981-82 home opener, Leafs 9, Chicago 8; OCT. 23, Nazareth; OCT. 29, Bob Dylan; NOV. 9, Frank Zappa; NOV. 13, Foreigner; NOV. 19, Black Sabbath; NOV. 23, Moody Blues; NOV. 24, Alice Cooper; DEC. 3, Barry Manilow; DEC. 6-7, Genesis; DEC. 10-11, AC/DC; DEC. 13, Blizzard indoor opener, def. Tampa 9-3; DEC. 17, Blizzard vs. New York; DEC. 31, Triumph.

89

JIM DOREY PENALTY RECORD

When rookie defenceman Jim Dorey's father drove down from Kingston to watch his son play at the Gardens for the first time, he should have asked for a seat near the penalty box.

His son's ice time was brief indeed as he racked up nine penalties—four minors, two majors, two misconducts and a game misconduct—during a 2-2 tie with Pittsburgh. When his total sentence was calculated at 48 minutes, it broke the NHL record of the day, remaining the most sins ever committed by a Toronto player in one game.

"My father didn't criticize me or anything, but he made me feel foolish," Dorey said. "He didn't see me play any hockey."

Dorey admitted his guilt in the first two penalties, but picked up the first misconduct for lipping off to the referee. Dorey fought Ken Schinkel and John Arbour, claiming both had started it.

Rather than being demoted for his actions as he feared, Dorey played until 1972 for the Leafs and later suited up for the Toronto Toros of the WHA.

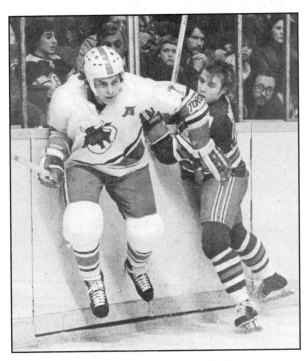

Toro, Toro, Toro: Toronto's "other" pro hockey team boasted Frank Mahovlich and penalty record holder Jim Dorey (above), among other ex-Leafs. (The Toronto Sun)

Gardens Gallery • Curtain Call

Before the age of video screens, the Gardens rigged up an alphalite message board high above both ends of the rink. Similar to the moving headline in New York's Times Square, it dissected a red curtain and flashed the scoring summary or tried to lead a crowd cheer.

"We called it the Travelling Sign, but it was such a pain to operate," recalled veteran Gardens fix-it man Paul Morris. One night after a Jim Dorey goal, someone hit the wrong key and the sign saluted Jim Dopey.

90

CLOSED CIRCUITS EVENTS

If the Gardens didn't host a world-class event, it accommodated thousands of fans with the big screen.

In the days before all-sports channels and pay TV, it was a Toronto tradition to watch a big title fight or a World Cup soccer match on the 40-foot wide, 30-foot high screen mounted at the North End. On other occasions, four screens were set up in the middle of the building.

"For its day, it wasn't a bad system," Paul Morris said.

But one of the most disappointing shows was September 8, 1974, when thousands came to watch daredevil Evel Knievel's feeble attempt to rocket himself over the Snake River Canyon.

"A puff of smoke and that was all," Morris said. "It was like Geraldo Rivera looking for Al Capone's treasure."

Hall-lelujah: When the closed circuit feed of a Muhammad Ali fight broke down, color sets were installed in the corridors for the 1970 bout. (Brian Willer/The Toronto Telegram)

Gardens Events—1982

JAN. 3, Blizzard vs. New York; JAN. 6, Blizzard vs. Chicago; JAN. 10, Blizzard vs. Tampa; JAN. 14, Blizzard v Tulsa; JAN. 21, Blizzard vs. Montreal; JAN. 24, Blizzard vs. Jacksonville; FEB. 2-7, Molson tennis; FEB. 14, Blizzard vs. Montreal; FEB. 19, Hall and Oates; MARCH 24, Rick Vaive first Leaf to score 50; MARCH 28, Rod Stewart; MARCH 17-18, Labatt Pro Skate; MARCH 30, Journey; MAY 7, Lover Boy; MAY 15, J. Geils Band; MAY 30, John Denver; JUNE 4, Ozzie Osborne; JUNE 14, The Commodores; JULY 27, Air Supply; JULY 29, Elton John; AUG. 2-3, Queen; SEPT, 23, Jethro Tull; SEPT. 24-25, Neil Diamond; SEPT. 28, ZZ Topp; OCT. 9, 1982-83 home opener, Leafs 5, Devils 5; OCT. 26, Van Halen; OCT. 28, Judas Priest; NOV. 8, Peter Gabriel; NOV. 9, Billy Joel; NOV. 15-17, Rush; DEC. 1, Pat Benetar; DEC. 5, Kenny Rogers (two shows); DEC. 6, Phil Collins; DEC. 9, Aerosmith; DEC. 16-17, The Who, DEC. 31, Saga.

Gardens Events—1983

JAN. 14, KISS; FEB. 8-13, Molson Pro Tennis; FEB. 18, Neil Young; MARCH 7, Hall and Oates; MARCH 20, Pro Skate; MARCH 29, Julio Inglesias; APRIL 19, Chris De Burgh; MAY 19, Roxy Music; MAY 25, Kinks; JUNE 10, Def Leopard/Krokus; AUG. 10, Robert Plant; AUG. 23, Lional Richie; SEPT. 25, Black Sabbath; OCT. 12, 1983-84 home opener, Leafs 4, Sabres 4; NOV. 6, United Way gala; NOV. 22-23, Genesis; DEC. 15, AC/DC.

GARDENS ARCHITECTURE

In 1989, when rumors were rife the Gardens was going to be drastically renovated, or perhaps torn down, Heritage Toronto came to its defence.

In addition to defining its place in Canadian hockey and its role as Toronto's largest assembly hall for 60 years, the group closely examined the Gardens' architecture and made some salient observations.

"The Gardens is one of the few examples of public architecture of the Depression era in Toronto," Heritage Toronto said in a report prepared for City Hall. "The form, structure, and interior space of the original building are all substantially intact.

"The design displays the vertical character, hard edges, recessed planes, vertical strip windows and low relief geometric ornament of the Art Deco with the horizontal banding and streamlined look of the Art Moderne, giving texture to the building's elevations."

The original front lobby.

Gardens Events—1984

FEB. 1-5, Molson Pro Tennis; MARCH 2, Saga; MARCH 4-5, Duran Duran; MARCH 15, KISS; APRIL 2, Judas Priest; APRIL 17, Van Halen; APRIL 25, Ozzie Osborne; APRIL 30, The Clash; JUNE 7, Air Supply; JULY 21, Chris de Burgh; JULY 28-29, Roger Waters; SEPT. 13, Elton John; SEPT. 21-22, Rush; OCT. 13, 1984-85 season opener, Leafs 4, Sabres 3; OCT. 23, Jethro Tull; NOV. 12, Cyndi Lauper; NOV. 15, Culture Club; NOV. 30, Iron Maiden; DEC., 2-3, Prince; DEC. 31, Platinum Blonde.

Gardens Events—1985

MARCH 14, Hall and Oates; MARCH 20, Kinks; MARCH 22, Chicago; MARCH 23, Roger Waters; MARCH 28, U2; APRIL 1, Deep Purple; APRIL 4, 11 Triumph; MAY 23, Madonna; AUG. 23, AC/DC; OCT. 12, 1985-86 home opener, Nordiques 4, Leafs 0; OCT. 18, Motley Crue; OCT. 21, Paul Young; OCT. 24, Supertramp; NOV. 8, Simple Minds; NOV. 12, Heart; NOV. 13, Howard Jones; NOV. 18, John Cougar Mellencamp; DEC. 2-3, ZZ Top; DEC. 6, Platinum Blonde; DEC. 31, Thompson Twins.

92

PAUL MORRIS

On those nights when the Leafs don't show up for work, there's no doubt announcer Paul Morris will.

He has not missed a home game since October 14, 1961, a 3-2 Leafs win over Boston. From a window in his northwest corner office, he's called every goal, assist and penalty and a few Leaf milestones, closing each night with friendly advice to "please drive and walk safely".

His streak is nearing 1,500 regular season and playoff games entering 1998-99.

"There are nights I've been sick and it's been a struggle," Morris once said.

"The streak is a source of pride, but I'm not going to be shattered if it comes to an end."

Longevity means nothing to Morris if you're not doing a proper job and observing P.A. etiquette. He doesn't doctor his decibels, unlike many other NHL cities where announcers sound like game show hosts and cheer goals.

Morris always has followed an old league directive that reads "announcers will refrain from personal comments on goals". He

laughs, figuring he's the only one who abides by it.

The rest of the week, Morris putters around the Gardens in his full-time role as head sound man. His office is in something of a time warp, with old equipment and various odds and ends parts interspersed with modern computers.

Morris had been at the Gardens since the 1940s, helping his father Doug, the building's innovative first superintendent, and announcing some Marlboro games. When Red Barber retired as Leafs announcer, Morris stepped in when no one else could be found.

He trips over the odd Russian or Slavic surname, but gets most frustrated at players who change the pronunciation of their own several times such as Walt Tkaczuk did.

Of all the big Leafs moments he has informed the building about, perhaps the greatest play he saw here had no goal or assist for him to announce. It came in the 1967 Cup final against Montreal.

"Dave Keon ragged the puck for a minute killing time and nobody touched him," Morris said.

Paul Morris

93

ORGAN MUSIC

In the early years of the Gardens, a bandshell existed in the south mezzanine.

Thirty musicians would play before the game and between periods, usually a jaunty military march to mark the Leafs' return to the ice.

That would change around 1956 when Smythe and building superintendent, Doug Morris, heard that the huge Wurlitzer organ at Shea's Hippodrome was to be a casualty of demolition to make room for the new City Hall at Queen and Bay.

The organ had fallen into neglect with the advent of talking pictures, and Horace Lapp, who played it in Shea's golden days was also displaced.

Morris, his son Paul and head Gardens sound man Bob Wood, hauled the monster back to Carlton St., and installed it above the bandshell.

Lapp came back to play, sometimes dropping by practice or just to surprise workers in quiet moments by pounding the keys. It was a stunt the elder Morris outlawed because he thought the heavy vibrations might shake some stonework loose.

Gardens Events—1986

JAN. 15-16, Torvill and Dean; MARCH 6-7, Rush; APRIL 4, Black Sabbath; APRIL 8, KISS; JULY 16, Eddie Murphy; SEPT. 12, Torvill and Dean; OCT. 3, Neil Young; OCT. 8, Kenny Rogers and Dolly Parton; OCT. 9, 1986-87 home opener, Leafs 7, Canadiens 4; OCT. 10, Stevie Wonder; OCT. 23-25, Bob Seger; OCT. 31, David Lee Roth; NOV. 11, Ochestral Manouvres In The Dark; NOV. 12-14, Lionel Richie; NOV. 21, Steve Winwood; NOV. 26-27, Peter Gabriel; DEC. 9, Metallica; DEC. 11, Billy Joel; DEC. 30, Kim Mitchell.

Gardens Events—1987

JAN. 9, Triumph; FEB. 26, Alice Cooper; FEB. 27, Paul Young; MARCH 19, Pretenders; MARCH 21-22, Iron Maiden; MARCH 23, Wrestlemania;APRIL 6; boxing, Marvin Hagler v Sugar Ray Leonard (CC); MAY 19, Chris De Burgh; JUNE 5, Psychedelic Furs; JUNE 19-21, Neil Diamond; JUNE 23-24, Paul Simon; JUNE 29, Bryan Adams; SEPT. 12, Level 42; OCT. 10, 1987-88 home opener, Leafs 5, Devils 2; OCT. 16, Heart; OCT. 19, Fleetwood Mac; OCT. 20, Aerosmith; OCT. 25, Motley Crue; NOV. 12 The Cars; NOV. 16, John Cougar Mellencamp; NOV. 19, Jethro Tull; DEC. 9, Yes; DEC. 10, KISS; DEC. 14, Depeche Mode.

Gardens Events—1988

FEB. 10, Supertramp; FEB. 12, Alice Cooper; FEB. 15, Sting; MARCH 7-8, Rush; APRIL 13, David Lee Roth; MAY 10, Robert Plant; AUG. 15, Amnesty International; AUG. 19, Scorpions; AUG. 23, Amy Grant; SEPT. 5, Prince; OCT. 7, Eric Clapton; OCT. 8, 1988-89 home opener, Leafs 7, Chicago 4; OCT. 13, AC/DC; OCT. 16 Midnight Oil; NOV. 18, Sounds United; NOV. 24, Rod Stewart.

94

FIRST TELEVISED GAME

This is one NHL "first" in which the Gardens must defer to the Montreal Forum. But in his book, *The Boys Of Saturday Night*, Scott Young points out that technically, Toronto did put a game on the air first in the spring of 1952.

During a Memorial Cup tilt between the Guelph Biltmores and Regina Pats, a mobile two-camera unit was set up for a closed-circuit broadcast, with Foster Hewitt calling play by play to a room full of advertising execs, CBC technicians and the men who would become the pioneers of Hockey Night In Canada.

However, such experiments had been bogged down by Smythe, who had little knowledge of the new medium, but demanded a say in the produc-

tion. He vowed that no paying customer would be blocked by a camera, therefore the equipment was first banished to the last row greys from where it was impossible to follow the play.

When Smythe was talked into moving the cameras closer to the ice, he wanted one on each side of the rink at the same height from the ice, but the CBC convinced him this would disorient viewers as the shot kept switching. A camera in the gondola was suggested so viewers could share Foster Hewitt's angle, but that too proved unfeasible.

By the time it was straightened out on November 1, 1952, CBC Montreal had been on the air with the Habs for three weeks.

Gardens Events—1989

FEB. 9-10, Neil Diamond; FEB. 13, Cheap Trick; FEB. 17, Tom Cochrane; FEB. 28, Chris De Burgh; MARCH 3, Sandi Patti; APRIL 7, Metallica; APRIL 12, REM; OCT. 11, 1989-90 home opener, Sabres 7, Leafs 1.

Gardens Events—1990

FEB. 6, Billy Joel; FEB. 11, Tears For Fears/Deborah Harry; MARCH 18, New Kids On The Block (two shows); MAY 16-17, Rush; OCT. 3. Robert Plant; OCT. 10, 1990-91 home opener, Nordiques 8, Leafs 5; OCT. 11, ZZ Top; OCT. 22, Judas Priest; NOV. 23, Heart/ Cheap Trick.

Gardens Events—1991

JAN. 16, Iron Maiden; FEB. 14, Neil, Young; MARCH 9, INXS; MARCH 21, Vanilla Ice; APRIL 13, Reba McEntire; SEPT. 14, Gloria Estefan; SEPT. 22, Tom Petty; OCT. 4, Garth Brooks; OCT. 5, 1991-92 home opener, Leafs 8, Wings 5; OCT. 22, George Michael; NOV. 12, Frank Sinatra; NOV. 14-15, Metallica; NOV. 28, Allman Brothers/Little Feat; DEC. 12, Luther Vandross; DEC. 16, Rush; DEC. 31, The Cult/Lenny Kravitz.

JOE THE JAIL GUARD

Do you ever wonder what Tiger Williams did to pass the time when serving some of his Leafs record 1,670 penalty minutes? At the Gardens, like hundreds of other Leaf and NHL sinners in the past 38 years, he'd gab away with Joe Lamantia.

"I usually talk to anyone who comes into the box, if they make the first move," the cheerful time-keeper says. "Tiger was a real gentleman, made it his business to talk to everybody."

But Lamantia does dislike being in the middle of the verbal warfare that goes on in the box after a fight or coincidental minors.

"That's the sad part," Lamantia said in 1987. "Players don't realize that parents with youngsters can hear them swearing. If they're arguing with the ref, I'll say, 'pipe down, your team needs you'."

Gardens Events—1992

JAN. 16, Bryan Adams; MARCH 3, Roxette; MARCH 19-20, Dire Straits; MARCH 24, U2; OCT. 6, 1992-93 home opener, Capitals 6, Leafs 5; OCT. 21, Def Leppard; NOV. 6, Billy Ray Cyrus; DEC. 1, Ministry.

Gardens Events—1993

JAN. 19, Placido Domingo; FEB. 13, Doug Gilmour's six -assist game; FEB. 25, Bon Jovi; MARCH 30, Prince; APRIL 24, Van Morrison; JUNE 14-16, Neil Diamond; JULY 11, WWF wrestling; SEPT. 22, Lenny Kravitz; OCT. 7, 1993-94 home opener, Leafs 6, Stars 3; OCT. 10, Gianni Morandi; OCT. 16, Lippizan Stallions; OCT. 20, Luther Vandross; OCT. 31, WWF wrestling; NOV. 4, Nirvana; NOV. 14, Macedonian Independance Day Parade; DEC. 5, Leafs Skills Challenge; Dec. 26. WWF wrestling.

Gardens Gallery • Banana Joe

Joe Lamantia, the Gardens longtime penalty timekeeper, isn't the sort who goes around ruining the careers of politicians. But he had an unwitting hand in torpedoing Robert Stanfield's aspirations as prime minister. It was during the federal Tories' leadership convention at the Gardens in 1967. The building was hot and noisy and the Gardens sent out for fruit, which Lamantia often supplied from his family market. Stanfield made the mistake of asking for a banana, holding it and eating it awkwardly while photographers snapped away. The banana and the new Conservative leader became inseparable as fodder for political cartoonists. Stanfield lost three times to Pierre Trudeau's Liberals in subsequent elections. Lamantia has been nicknamed Banana Joe ever since.

THE ICE

An arena that calls itself the class of the league should have the best ice, and the Gardens maintained an excellent reputation from opening night through its busiest years as a multi-purpose facility.

Credit the late chief engineer Doug Moore, who pioneered a process called Jet Ice, a necessity in an era when TV lights, late spring playoff games and quick conversions from concerts require a durable sheet.

Jet Ice, achieved after seven years of study with help from chemist Gil Adamson, is essentially de-ionized water. It produces a harder, three-quarter inch covering of the 85-by-200 foot playing surface (26 metres by 61 metres).

The two- to three-day procedure begins with a few millimetres of water on the concrete floor, frozen by pumping minus-25 degree celcius brine (calcium chloride), through 23 kilometres of pipes beneath the floor.

Hundreds of gallons of white paint are added, then more water for a clear contrast between the ice and the black puck. The lines and faceoff circles are then painted on.

Moore's prayers were answered in 1983 when the original floor and pipes were finally torn out, giving the Gardens a chance to compete with Edmonton's Northlands Coliseum, which is still generally considered to have the league's best ice.

Pipe Dreams: The miles of pipe that made the Gardens the best ice surface in the league for years were torn up in 1983. (Lee Lamonte/The Toronto Sun)

Gardens Events—1994

JAN. 22, Billy Joel; JAN. 25, Canada - USA Olympic hockey; FEB. 20, WWF wrestling; MARCH 2-6, Dorothy Hamill's Ice Capades; MARCH 11, Rock and Roll All-Stars; MARCH 13, Canadian University hockey finals; APRIL 15, Stars On Ice; MAY 7, Rush; MAY 11, Eros Ramazzotti; MAY 21, Star Nite '94; MAY 29, ZZ Top; JUNE 18, Pantera; JUNE 26, WWF wrestling; AUG. 4-11, world basketball championships; AUG. 21, WWF wrestling; SEPT. 11, Megastars '94; SEPT. 23, Elvis Stojko Ice Show; OCT. 5-6, Eric Clapton; OCT. 23, WWF Hart Attack Tour; OCT. 29, Maple Leafs open house; NOV. 23-27, Moscow Circus; NOV. 29, Torvill and Dean; DEC. 1, Nine Inch Nails.

97

TIME MACHINE

The Gardens had the first four-faced time clock in pro sports and the first solid state digital timer.

The first clock to hang above the Gardens was a 3½-ton, four-faced monster, likely assembled by a shipbuilding firm in Thunder Bay, Ontario.

But with age, the gears constantly wore out, causing the minute hand to drag on the way up. It was getting so hard to keep accurate time on it by the 1960s, that a system of lights were wired to the control room to keep count of the clock's revolutions.

Sports timers with mechanical relays had been invented by the mid-1960s, but technicians Paul Morris and Bob Wood thought they could create something much better than what was on the market.

The original clock (left) and the scoreboard that served the Gardens from 1966 to 1982. (The Toronto Sun)

Over a two-year period they designed and assembled the famous green Dominion clock right in the Gardens. It incorporated time, score and penalties, with the intense heat of the bulbs allowed to escape through perforated metal and the entire clock angled to allow rinkside patrons a full view.

A smaller module would drop down from the main clock with fan-

blown flags of Canada and the U.S. for national anthems.

A new clock was erected in 1983, at a cost of $1.5 million with 40,000 red, green, blue and white bulbs and four screens that are 18 metres wide. A further $1-million upgrade was made in 1996. By contrast, the new video scoreboard at the Air Canada Centre will cost close to $5 million.

The $1 million scoreboard installed in 1982. (Ken Kerr/The Toronto Sun)

Gardens Events—1995

JAN. 21, Reggae Superfest; JAN. 25, 1995 home opener, Leafs 6, Canucks 2; FEB. 4, Megadeth; FEB. 10, Tragically Hip; FEB. 12, Oldtimers Hockey Challenge; MARCH 10, Amy Grant; MARCH 12, Canadian University hockey finals; MARCH 16, Black Crowes; MARCH 17, Tom Petty; MARCH 18, WWF wrestling; APRIL 21-22, Stars On Ice; MAY 16, Beastie Boys; MAY 20, Hollywood Megastars; JUNE 25, Van Morrison; AUG. 10, Concerto D'Autunno; SEPT. 9, Madhuri Dixit; SEPT. 17, WWF wrestling; SEPT. 29, Elvis Stojko's Tour of Champions; OCT. 25, Green Day; NOV. 12, Dalla Morandi.

Gardens Events—1996

JAN. 7, Leafs Skills Challenge; FEB. 6, Lenny Kravitz; FEB. 15, Canadian Hockey League Chrysler Cup; FEB. 17, Oldtimers Hockey Challenge; MARCH 8, Bob Seger; MARCH 10, Canadian University hockey finals; MARCH 18, Melissa Etheridge; APRIL 14, Concerto Di Primavera; APRIL 19-20, Stars On Ice; APRIL 28, Rangeele Dilwale; JUNE 29, Garden Party IV; SEPT. 14, Smashing Pumpkins; SEPT. 21, Pearl Jam; SEPT. 27, Blue Rodeo; OCT. 4, Elvis Stojko's Tour Of Champions; OCT. 5, 1996-97 home opener, Leafs 4, Ducks 1; DEC. 12-13, Tragically Hip.

Gardens Gallery • Igloo Takes Over

When the Gardens is abandoned in February 1999, it will surrender the title of the NHL's oldest building, which it held following completion of new arenas in Montreal, Boston and Chicago in the mid-1990s. The "new" old building in the league becomes the Civic Arena in Pittsburgh, or the Igloo as it's known, which was opened in 1961. It was designed primarily as a theatre, with a retractable roof that has rarely been opened.

98

BALLARD BUNKER

The Gardens was Harold Ballard's castle, the bunker his royal box.

For almost 20 years, Ballard and King Clancy were a fixture in this Northeast perch, a pair of gargoyles as Saturday Night's David Macfarlane described them. They were also compared to the grumpy old muppets, Statler and Waldorf.

When Clancy died in 1986, a shaken Ballard ordered the bunker draped with black curtains and closed for good. But unable to watch the games comfortably anywhere else, the octogenarian went back inside.

After Ballard's death in 1990, the box was turned over to the Leafs' alumni.

King and Harold: King Clancy (left) and Harold Ballard watch a game from the bunker. (The Toronto Sun)

Gardens Gallery • Tiger Tales

When Ballard bought the CFL's Hamilton Tiger-Cats for $1.2 million in 1978, he ordered the club's logo painted on the ice and the boards. Tiger Williams made a point of tapping each tabby every time he scored, but the paint job broke an NHL rule of the day forbidding advertising. At first, Ballard ignored the threat of fines from president John Ziegler, while the Boston Bruins got in on the act one night by unfurling two Toronto Argonaut flags on their bench during the national anthems. Eventually Ballard scrapped the Tiger-Cats artwork.

99

OTHER EVENTS

To detail each of the incredibly wide variety of games, meetings, shows, speeches and events that have taken place at the Gardens would defy space in this book. But here are some examples that escaped mention elsewhere:

Aquatics, ballet, beauty contests, Boy Scout/ Girl Guide Jamborees, bull riding, car shows, charity skates, conventions, curling, equestrian, ethnic dancing, flea markets, floor hockey, gymnastics, lectures, minor hockey, model airplane shows, piano ensembles, roller derby, Shakespeare, softball, tae-kwon do, volleyball, and world basketball championships.

Exercise Yard: The Gardens is put to use as a gym for training camp in 1980. (The Toronto Sun)

Gardens Events—1997

FEB. 7, Oldtimer's Hockey Challenge; FEB. 9, Leafs Skills Challenge; FEB. 12, CHL Chrysler Cup; FEB. 14, NBA, Raptors vs. Milwaukee; FEB. 16, Raptors vs. Detroit; MARCH 15, Ice Capades (two shows); MARCH 17, Canadian University hockey finals; MARCH 18, Raptors vs. Philadelphia; MARCH 29, Backstreet Boys; APRIL 13, Punjabi Super Show; APRIL 17 Bush X; APRIL 18-19, Stars On Ice; MAY 4-5, Lords Of The Dance; MAY 12, No Doubt; JUNE 1, Megastars; JUNE 15, Tunes Of Glory Military Tattoo; SEPT. 19, Elvis Stojko Tour Of Champions; SEPT. 28, Team Canada '72 Reunion Game; OCT. 1, 1997-98 home opener, Capitals 4, Leafs 1; NOV. 1, HollyWoof (two shows); NOV. 9, Andre Rieu.

Gardens Events—1998

JAN. 3-4, Holiday circus; JAN. 15, Oasis; JAN. 17, Our Lady Peace; FEB. 8, Oldtimer's Hockey Challenge; FEB. 10, CHL Chrysler Cup; FEB. 13, Bryan Adams; FEB. 20, OHL, St. Michael's Majors vs. Barrie; FEB. 21, Leafs Skills Challenge; FEB. 22, St. Michael's vs. Barrie; FEB. 25, Scotland The Brave; MARCH 20, Shaolin Monks; MARCH 31, NBA, Raptors vs. Los Angeles Lakers; APRIL 2, Andre Rieu; APRIL 4, Eros Ramazzotti; APRIL 12, Radiohead; APRIL 18, Megastars; APRIL 19, Raptors vs. Philadelphia; OCT. 10, 1998-99 season opener, Leafs vs. Detroit; OCT. 29, Bob Dylan; NOV. 17, Dave Matthews Band; NOV. 15, Neil Diamond, NOV. 20, Elvis Stojko Tour of Champions.

Gardens Events—1999

FEB. 13, Blackhawks at Leafs (Gardens closes).

100

FUTURE OF THE GARDENS

The days of Leafs hockey at the Gardens will soon be over, but the spirited debate on the building's fate should rage for years.

For the moment, the plan is to keep it for the St. Michael's Juniors, perhaps the IHL, AHL or just as a Leafs practice rink.

Club president Ken Dryden wants minor hockey, oldtimers and women's hockey to use the Gardens, at least to justify the cost of keeping the ice-plant running.

Chairman Steve Stavro has insisted that the Gardens, which will turn 68 in November of 1999, is "a shrine" that will not be demolished.

As a designated historical building, the wrecking ball would be fought by City Hall. But the urge to utilize the building year-round in some kind of venture eventually may win the day.

As long as the building's facade is preserved,

Ice Jam: One of the many charity skates at the Gardens. More are planned with the Leafs moving out as a way to keep the building open. (The Toronto Sun)

ideas have ranged from a new home for the Hockey Hall Of Fame, to a hotel, a convention centre, a movie complex, opera house, concert hall or casino.

An ambitious suggestion was to use its vast space to create a Toronto version of Marineland, with killer whales cavorting in a big pool where centre ice is now.

"Whatever they do, it'll always be the Gardens to us," Hall of Fame goaltender Johnny Bower said.

Brian Conacher, the former Leaf and building vice-president whose father Charlie scored the first goal in Gardens history, favored a restoration project in tandem with its 1930s roots.

"I'd like to see it preserved in some way," longtime captain George Armstrong said. "Conn Smythe would not have wanted it to stay empty."

Other Titles By Sports Publishing Inc.

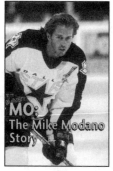

Mo:
The Mike Modano Story
by Mike Modano with John Sanful

Dallas Stars forward Mike Modano is one of the most successful American-born hockey players in the National Hockey League. As a teenage sensation, Modano was the most heralded player for the Prince Albert Raiders, eventually becoming only the second American drafted first overall by the Minnesota North Stars in 1988. In nine years he has been transformed from a skinny, wide-eyed rookie to an exciting one-on-one player with game-breaking abilities. Follow the career of Modano from the cold winters as a boy in Westland, Michigan, to the hot days in the Texas sun as he leads the Stars to the Stanley Cup.

1998 • 200 pp • 16-page photo section • 6 x 9 hardcover • ISBN 1-58261-014-2 • $22.95

The Greatest Players and Moments of the Philadelphia Flyers
by Stan Fischler

Stan Fischler, one of the most respected and accomplished authors in hockey history, is set to release his first book for Sports Publishing, Inc. — *The Greatest Players and Moments of the Philadelphia Flyers*. The Flyers have been one of hockey's most successful and popular teams in recent memory with an appearance in the 1997 Stanley Cup Finals and a roster filled with stars like John LeClair, Ron Hextall, Paul Coffey, and Eric Lindros. Boasting Hall of Famers like Bernie Parent, Bobby Clarke, and Bill Barber, the Flyers also are rich in history and tradition. Relive the memories of the 35-game unbeaten streak, the back-to-back Stanley Cups in mid-1970s and the legend of the Broad Street Bullies in this beautiful hardcover offering.

1988 • 250 pp • 150+ photos • 8 1/2 x 11 hardcover • ISBN 1-57167-234-6 • $29.95

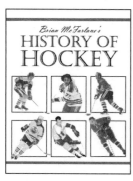

Brian McFarlane's History of Hockey
by Brian McFarlane

Here is the heart and soul of hockey—the story of more than a century of the world's fastest sport. From its beginnings on lonely winter ponds in Canada, the game of ice hockey has been transformed into the world's most demanding and exhilarating team sport, played before tens of thousands of fans by skilled and powerful professionals under the archlights of great and legendary sports temples.

In *Brian McFarlane's History of Hockey*, Brian McFarlane, one of the game's most respected and recognized commentators for "Hockey Night in Canada", retells hockey's history in a fast-moving year-by-year account of the game's origins, rule changes, great games, plays and trades in both regular season and playoff action. He traces the fortunes of the sport's most successful and enduring dynasties, fly-by-night organizations and all of the major teams and leagues, their heroes, workhorses and players of infamy.

Written with the knowledge and insight of a life spent playing and following the game, McFarlane has amassed more hockey information in *Brian McFarlane's History of Hockey* than exists in any other book of its kind.

Colorful, anecdotal, up-to-date and complete, *Brian McFarlane's History of Hockey* contains all of the hockey events worthy of being remembered or destined never to be forgotten.

1997 • 400 pp • 8 1/2 x 11 hardcover • ISBN 1-57167-145-5 • $34.95

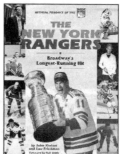

The New York Rangers: Broadway's Longest-Running Hit
by John Kreiser and Lou Friedman

After 70 years of waiting, New York City's hockey fans finally have a book about their beloved Rangers. In *The New York Rangers: Broadway's Longest-Running Hit,* Ranger fans can savor the legendary feats of such star skaters as Ed Giacomin, Brad Park, Andy Bathgate, Rod Gilbert and Mark Messier. Each of the 70 easy-to-read, four-page chapters reveal tidbits about Ranger hockey never before available in book form. The New York Rangers and Madison Square Garden have opened up their archives to reveal numerous rarely published photographs. If you like browsing through record sections, you've never seen anything like this one. Authors John Kreiser and Lou Friedman and NHL editor John Halligan have developed a book that is sure to become a collector's item.

1996 • 400 pp • 12-page color photo section • 8 1/2 x 11 hardcover • ISBN 1-57167-041-6 • $39.95

www.SportsPublishingInc.com